David Bonham-Carter

BUILDING
SELF-ESTEEM
A FIVE-POINT PLAN
FOR VALUING YOURSELF MORE

ICON

Published in the UK in 2016 by
Icon Books Ltd, Omnibus Business Centre,
39–41 North Road, London N7 9DP
email: info@iconbooks.com
www.iconbooks.com

First published in the UK in 2012 by Icon Books Ltd

Sold in the UK, Europe and Asia
by Faber & Faber Ltd, Bloomsbury House,
74–77 Great Russell Street,
London WC1B 3DA or their agents

Distributed in the UK, Europe and Asia
by Grantham Book Services,
Trent Road, Grantham NG31 7XQ

Distributed in Australia and New Zealand
by Allen & Unwin Pty Ltd,
PO Box 8500, 83 Alexander Street,
Crows Nest, NSW 2065

Distributed in South Africa by
Jonathan Ball, Office B4, The District,
41 Sir Lowry Road, Woodstock 7925

Distributed in India by Penguin Books India,
7th Floor, Infinity Tower – C, DLF Cyber City,
Gurgaon 122002, Haryana

Distributed in Canada by Publishers Group Canada,
76 Stafford Street, Unit 300
Toronto, Ontario M6J 2S1

Distributed in the USA
by Publishers Group West
1700 Fourth St., Berkeley, CA, 94710

ISBN: 978-184831-960-8

Typeset in Adobe Caslon by Marie Doherty

Printed and bound in the UK by Clays Ltd, St Ives plc

About the author

David Bonham-Carter is a life coach and writer on self-help topics who specializes in helping people struggling with self-esteem, anxiety, assertiveness and related difficulties. For many years David worked in the UK as a social worker helping people from a range of backgrounds to achieve positive changes in their lives through face-to-face work before setting up his own life coaching practice in Bristol. He has a Masters Degree in Social Work from the University of Kent (passed with distinction) and a Masters Degree in Philosophy from the University of Bristol. He has a particular interest in the use of cognitive behavioural therapy (CBT) techniques for helping people to develop self-esteem and assertiveness skills and he has written a number of guides to dealing with particular emotional and cognitive difficulties. More information about his life coaching service and his practical self-help guides is available at his website: www.davidbonham-carter.com.

David would like to thank Denise for her incisive and helpful comments on the first draft of the book.

'It is the mind that maketh good or ill,
That maketh wretch or happy, rich or poor.'
—Edmund Spenser,
The Faerie Queene, Book VI, Canto IX

Contents

Introduction:
The journey to self-esteem

SELF-ESTEEM AND ATTITUDES TO THE SELF

As human beings we make judgements all the time about the world we live in, the situations we are involved in and the people we come into contact with. If you have low self-esteem you make negative judgements *about yourself* much of the time. You feel that you are not good enough or that you do not act well enough. Self-esteem is therefore intimately connected with self-perception and goes to the core of your identity. In this book I aim to present you with some helpful ideas on self-esteem and dealing with negative thoughts about yourself, in a format that is informative and practical.

Different traditions and cultures have produced their own accounts of self-consciousness and desirable attitudes to take towards the self: the Chinese sage Lao Tzu counselled in the Tao Te Ching that mastering the self requires strength, the ancient Greek philosopher Socrates urged: 'Know thyself', and René Descartes ushered in modern Western philosophy with the famous observation 'I think therefore I am.' Ideas from Hindu and Buddhist philosophical approaches and meditation techniques for observing yourself or 'letting go' of thoughts have also been adapted by recent American and British self-help authors to help with self-esteem and other issues.

A NEW APPROACH TO SELF-ESTEEM –
A FIVE-POINT PLAN

To provide a new approach to self-esteem that is easy to follow, I have separated out the aspects of developing self-esteem into five key points, or ingredients, each of which has a chapter devoted to it. Together the first letters of each of the five key ingredients combine to form the word VALUE:

Value yourself
Accept yourself
Look after yourself
Understand yourself
Empower yourself

Chapter 1 on *valuing yourself* covers techniques that you can use for building a positive self-image and techniques for countering limiting beliefs that may be inhibiting you from developing your potential.

Chapter 2 on *accepting yourself* covers techniques that you can use to help you develop an attitude of self-acceptance, both in putting negative thoughts about yourself in particular situations in perspective and in dealing with an overall sense of inadequacy, if that is something you experience.

Chapter 3 on *looking after yourself* considers an area which is sometimes undervalued in discussions of self-esteem – that of taking good care of your mind and body. This is important because your mental and physical health are often intimately connected.

In **chapter 4** on *understanding yourself* I start by examining potential causes of low self-esteem and move from there into illustrating how you can develop your own understanding and awareness of yourself, your identity and your personality in healthy ways that help to address negative voices from your past or present.

Chapter 5 on *empowering yourself* brings you forward into the arena of developing your assertiveness and improving related communication skills in relationships.

The book's conclusion then provides you with suggestions as to how you can build on the most relevant parts of what you have learned from the VALUE acronym by developing it into a purposeful plan for you to use.

A PRACTICAL PLAN FOR BUILDING SELF-ESTEEM

The book is written as a practical guide. In each chapter I provide tips for you to follow and exercises to try out to help you develop the aspect of self-esteem that is being discussed. I also provide case studies to illustrate how individuals in particular situations might apply the techniques. In compiling the case studies I have drawn on my professional experience as a life coach working with people around self-esteem, as well as on my own personal experience and relationships. The people in the case studies are not real individuals, but their dilemmas and efforts reflect concerns and approaches that are common among people that I have worked with or know.

Most of the exercises and techniques that I describe in the book follow a problem-solving approach. I discuss an issue that can create difficulties for your self-esteem, then explain techniques that you can use to help you deal with that issue in a constructive way, illustrating how to apply the techniques through the case studies.

COGNITIVE BEHAVIOURAL THERAPY (CBT)

We are living in an exciting period in the field of self-development. In recent times there has been a sea change in therapeutic approaches, with many people rejecting the old psychoanalytical accounts of what drives people's actions and feelings in favour of practical, research-based psychological therapies that focus on addressing negative, distorted or disempowering thoughts in a constructive way.

The approaches that I describe in this book for each of the five key ingredients of self-esteem covered in my

VALUE acronym draw heavily on the ideas of one of the most well-known of the modern practical approaches to therapy and self-help: cognitive behavioural therapy – or CBT as it is popularly known. CBT rests on the belief that how we think influences our actions and our feelings, and that by correcting or modifying distorted, erroneous or exaggerated beliefs we can achieve more balanced feelings. There is a substantial body of research suggesting that CBT is particularly helpful for a range of issues that involve negative thinking patterns, such as anxiety and depression. Low self-esteem can be a factor in depression, and you can apply CBT techniques purposefully to help deal with it.

Fortunately, CBT is not rocket science. In this book I hope to show you how its insights and practical ideas, along with other helpful tools and concepts, can be used to shed light on the issues associated with self-esteem and can also be used to build your self-esteem and keep in perspective the problems that are related to low self-esteem.

In the journey towards a reasonable level of self-esteem we will touch on a number of different ideas about what self-esteem is and what is most important in addressing it. Some of the contributors to the debate about the nature of self-esteem emphasize one aspect of it at the expense of another, which you will see if you investigate any of the resources suggested for further reading at the end of this book. In this book I have sought to present important ideas on self-esteem in a way that forms a coherent whole based on the five key elements of the VALUE acronym. My aim has been to try to illustrate ideas and theories simply and clearly to show how they can be of immediate practical use, providing a route to follow if you are interested in enhancing your own self-esteem or if you are a professional working with people to develop their self-esteem.

try it now

The first step on your journey is to assess your current self-esteem. You can find a number of different assessment tools to help with this. One of the most well known is the Rosenberg Self-Esteem Scale. Answer the questions in it to start the process of reflecting on or developing your self-esteem:

THE ROSENBERG SELF-ESTEEM SCALE

Below is a list of statements dealing with your general feelings about yourself. For each statement, if you strongly agree, circle SA. If you agree, circle A. If you disagree, circle D. If you strongly disagree, circle SD.

1. 'I feel that I'm a person of worth, at least on an equal plane with others.'

   SA   A   D   SD

2. 'I feel that I have a number of good qualities.'

   SA   A   D   SD

3. 'All in all, I am inclined to feel that I am a failure.'

SA   A   D   SD

4. 'I am able to do things as well as most other people.'

SA   A   D   SD

5. 'I feel I do not have much to be proud of.'

SA   A   D   SD

6. 'I take a positive attitude toward myself.'

SA   A   D   SD

7. 'On the whole I am satisfied with myself.'

SA   A   D   SD

8. 'I wish I could have more respect for myself.'

SA   A   D   SD

9. 'I certainly feel useless at times.'

SA   A   D   SD

10. 'At times I think I am no good at all.'

SA   A   D   SD

Source: Rosenberg, Morris. 1989. *Society and the Adolescent Self-Image*. Revised edition. Middletown, CT: Wesleyan University Press.

Devised by Dr Morris Rosenberg, the scale was initially used to assess the self-esteem of a sample group of over 5,000 high school students in New York. Since then it has been widely used in a range of settings and locations with a variety of different user groups, including both adults and children, male and female participants.

In the appendix (see pages 207–8), you can find instructions for scoring your answers to the Rosenberg Self-Esteem Scale.

If you have achieved reasonable scores in the Rosenberg Self-Esteem Scale then it may be that you do not urgently need to follow any of the ideas in this book for yourself. Nonetheless, what follows may help you to deepen your understanding of self-esteem and of the issues that others struggle with in their lives.

On the other hand, if you are not happy with your scores on the Rosenberg Scale, you may well find some of the ideas that follow help you directly. In that case, it's time to move on to chapter 1 where we consider the first point in the VALUE plan for developing self-esteem: valuing yourself.

CHAPTER 1

Value yourself

'If you hear a voice within you say
"You cannot paint", then by all means
paint, and that voice will be silenced.'

—Vincent Van Gogh

AIMING FOR A REASONABLE LEVEL OF SELF-ESTEEM
Self-esteem is bound up in the feelings and thoughts that you have about yourself, your worth, your abilities and your qualities.

The degree to which you might generally value yourself, your abilities and your actions can fall into one of the three categories below:

1. Person with low self-esteem
- You don't consider that you have much worth

- You doubt your abilities

- You feel that you do not have many qualities or that those you do have are unimportant

- You are not satisfied with yourself

- You rarely give yourself credit for anything you do.

2. Person with reasonable level of self-esteem

- You feel that you have worth and also recognize other people as having worth

- You recognize the abilities and qualities you have without exaggerating them

- You honestly acknowledge areas where you are not so able

- You are proud of some things you have done and you regret some things.

3. Arrogant or conceited person

- You think that you have a lot of worth, more than other people

- You think that you have a lot of abilities and qualities – and you may exaggerate them

- You don't recognize or acknowledge failings or you minimize them

- You may dismiss other people's views or have little regard for them

- You may find it difficult to take reasonable criticism.

If you fall into category 1 or feel that a number of its characteristics apply to you, then this book is for you. We will focus on how someone with a low level of self-esteem can bring themself up to a reasonable level of self-esteem.

PSEUDO SELF-ESTEEM

There are differences of opinion about whether a person who falls within category 3 (arrogant or conceited) should be considered as having a high level of self-esteem or not. Some people regard arrogant and conceited people as having a very high level of self-esteem because they have a high opinion of their abilities and worth – a view which is supported by much of the research that has been done around self-esteem. On the other hand, there are also respected writers in the field of self-esteem such as Nathaniel Branden, author of the book *The Six Pillars of Self-Esteem*, who would probably regard conceited and arrogant people as having 'pseudo self-esteem', suggesting that their conceit masks doubts about their self-worth and that their arrogance is really a protective cover for insecurity rather than being genuine self-esteem.

Having a reasonable level of self-esteem (category 2) is, I would suggest, where most people (including myself) would want to be. As the word 'reasonable' suggests, it is not about perfection, it is about *balance*, recognizing and appreciating the positives in your life while also being prepared to honestly acknowledge areas where you might improve.

PROBLEMS ASSOCIATED WITH LOW SELF-ESTEEM

Research suggests that if you have low self-esteem it can increase your risk of:

- Depression

- Suicide or suicide attempts

- Eating disorders

- Teenage pregnancy for young women

- Lower earnings and extended unemployment for young men

- Being victimized by others.

There is also evidence to suggest that if your self-esteem is higher:

- You have a better chance of establishing and maintaining successful relationships.

- You are more likely to persist after experiencing an initial failure in attempting something, i.e. you are likely to be better at sustaining your motivation.

CAN YOU HAVE TOO MUCH SELF-ESTEEM?

There is some research that suggests that people who participate in potentially dangerous activities such as driving too fast or after having consumed too much alcohol may statistically be more likely to have high self-esteem than low self-esteem, and that people involved in delinquency or violent crime may also be more likely to have high self-esteem than low self-esteem. This may be related to the point made above that high self-esteem can merge into arrogance or conceit, or a lack of respect for others. At any rate, it seems to back up my suggestion that a sensible aim is to have a *reasonable* level of self-esteem and a degree of balance, rather than to have high self-esteem to the point of arrogance.

BENEFITS OF A REASONABLE LEVEL OF SELF-ESTEEM

I would suggest that some of the potential benefits of having a *reasonable* level of self-esteem as compared to the two alternatives are as follows:

Advantages of having a reasonable level of self-esteem compared to having a low level of self-esteem:

- You feel better about yourself.

- You don't have to worry so much about whether you are doing the right thing or whether you are good enough.

- You can engage in relationships constructively without putting yourself down.

- You feel comfortable enough in yourself and confident enough to communicate effectively.

- You are more likely to be able to assert yourself effectively without worrying excessively about what others think.

- You find it easier to focus on the present and concentrate on tasks in hand because you are less anxious.

- You can use your energy constructively instead of being preoccupied by how well you are doing or how you appear to others.

Advantages of having a reasonable level of self-esteem compared to being arrogant and conceited:

- You are better able to sustain genuine relationships because you treat others with respect.

- You are more likely to communicate in a reasonable way rather than to dismiss others' views unfairly.

- You have a greater ability to work in partnership with others and to learn from others.

- You are better able to assess your actions and abilities honestly and therefore you have better prospects of improving and developing yourself.

- You are more likely to be genuinely respected by others.

THE SUBJECTIVITY OF SELF-ESTEEM

Statistics and research give us some ideas of the benefits of having a reasonable level of self-esteem but not every individual is exactly the same. You may find that some of the benefits suggested above are particularly important and relevant for you, or you may find that there are other reasons, not captured in the above, why it will be helpful for you to have a more balanced level of self-esteem.

try it now

On a sheet of paper, write down what you think will be the main benefits of having a reasonable level of self-esteem *for you*. You can keep your list to hand as you try out some of the ideas in this book, as a motivational tool and reminder of why you are trying to make changes in the way you act and think. You can also refer back to your list after a period of time to help you reflect on whether particular changes you have made have helped. If they have, then continue them. If not, then reflect on why not and adapt or adjust them suitably.

WHERE TO START IF YOU WANT TO IMPROVE YOUR SELF-ESTEEM

Whether you have had low self-esteem since an early age or your self-esteem has fallen due to life circumstances or particular events, you may be able to think of times when your self-esteem was a little better than it is now. Was there anything you were doing differently then that you are not doing now? If so, consider trying to start doing something similar again. Alternatively, if part of the reason why you now feel worse and your self-esteem is lower relates to a change in your circumstances or life events, then ask yourself what would be a different way that you could react to that change to help your self-esteem.

case study
MARY: REMEMBERING WHAT WORKS AND DOING IT AGAIN
Mary has experienced low self-esteem since as far back as she can remember. When she was a child, she was frequently told by her parents that she wasn't doing things right and she developed a feeling that she was not good enough. However, on reflecting about times when she felt better about herself, she remembers a period when she was exercising regularly and was also involved in doing different activities on a regular basis. She decides to join a fitness session for women at the local leisure centre once a week and also starts attending a local singing group, as she enjoyed singing in her school choir when younger. She finds that both activities help to take her out of herself. Doing something that she feels is worthwhile raises her spirits and she starts to feel better about herself and her situation.

case study
ROBERT: CHANGING YOUR REACTION TO EVENTS
When he was younger Robert had a bright, confident personality. He obtained a high-powered job in his mid-twenties working for

a large company in London. After a few years a new boss came into the company who was very demanding and highly critical of Robert's work. Robert began to enjoy his work less and stresses mounted, but he kept on with the work for another three years as he had a young family to support. He started to look for alternative posts but only had limited time to do so. One year the pressure and stresses mounted as the firm began the launch of a new project. On a particularly stressful day, after working late Robert made a relatively minor error for which his boss heavily criticized him. This was the trigger for Robert. He went home and, after discussing it with his wife, decided to resign even though he didn't have a post to go to. Unfortunately, shortly after his resignation, Robert fell ill and was unable to look for work for several months, during which time he started to blame himself for having given up his job. His belief in himself and his self-esteem fell and at times he began to think that maybe the illness was some kind of punishment for his own shortcomings.

Recently Robert has decided to try to react in a different way to the change in circumstances. Each time that he is tempted to blame himself for what has happened, he reminds himself that actually he discussed resigning with his wife and she agreed, and that he couldn't have foreseen that he would get ill. Rather than dwell on what might have been, he now consciously tries not to be so hard on himself and to focus on what he can sensibly do in his current situation. He also reminds himself that he wasn't happy in his work. He talks about his options with his wife and they decide that when he recovers he will try to look for something in a different field of work, even if it is less well paid. This more balanced attitude helps him to cope with his illness and to feel better about himself and his situation. He still sees his situation as unpleasant but he also now sees it as giving him the opportunity to reflect on what is important to him and his family and on how he can try to set personal goals which are relevant to that.

ENJOYING YOURSELF

Valuing yourself involves creating some space and time to do things that you enjoy doing. This could be almost anything legal and non-harmful. It could for example include any of the following:

- Listening to music

- Reading and/or writing

- Sports

- Cooking

- Meeting friends

- Helping people

- Self-development activities or research

- Gardening

- Walking

- Playing with your children (if you have children) or contributing to their life

- Watching a good film

- Having a laugh
- Travelling
- Painting
- Looking at scenery
- Finding out about new things
- Working on a particular project or in a role you value or enjoy
- Campaigning for a good cause.

Of course, the above list is not exhaustive. It is just to give a few possible ideas and stimulate you into your own thoughts about your own personal preferences for enjoyable activities – which may be very different!

REMEMBER
Give yourself permission to do some things that you enjoy doing. This is one of the first rules of self-esteem. I am not talking here about harmful activities or actions that might cause problems for you or others. I am talking about ordinary, everyday pursuits or pastimes that you can enjoy or find rewarding.

try it now

Write down ten activities that you enjoy doing currently or have enjoyed in the past.

Ten things that I enjoy doing:

1. ....

2. ....

3. ....

4. ....

5. ....

6. ....

7. ....

8. ....

9. ....

10. ....

Commit to doing one thing on your list for one hour within the next two days if you can, or if that is not possible, then do it as soon as possible after the next two days.

RECOGNIZING YOUR POSITIVES

Doing some things that you enjoy can help you to feel better about yourself and your situation. It can also serve an additional purpose:

If you suffer from low self-esteem then you are likely to find it much easier to remember your (perceived) negative characteristics and unsuccessful actions than to acknowledge your qualities, abilities or achievements. Even if you do recognize some positives about yourself or your life, you may discount them, minimizing their significance or value or not taking much personal credit for them even when it is due.

If you have a mindset which leads you instinctively to focus on your negatives rather than your positives then you may need some help to balance that process. You can use the exercise that you have just completed – identifying things that you enjoy doing – as a springboard to help you identify and acknowledge some of your positive features.

The way to do this is to look through your list and identify what abilities, qualities and achievements you demonstrate when you do any of the things that you enjoy. Remember that the abilities and qualities *don't* have to be achievements that meet a standard set by others. For example the following are qualities:

- Enthusiasm

- Determination

- A sense of humour

- Kindness

- Patience.

case study JOANNA: ACKNOWLEDGING WHAT YOU ARE PROUD OF INSTEAD OF TRYING TO MEET EXTERNAL OR IMAGINARY STANDARDS

Joanna finds it difficult to identify any positives in herself, her achievements or qualities. She married at 26 and at that time decided to give up her prospects of a career as a lawyer to concentrate on bringing up her family while her husband worked. She and her husband divorced when their children were aged eight and ten and she continued with the childcare responsibilities without much help. Now, in middle age, when she tries to make a list of her achievements and qualities, she finds it difficult to do at first because she can only think of the fact that her marriage didn't last and that she did not continue her early career. However, when she makes a list of things she enjoys doing or that she enjoyed doing in the past, she is able to see that they demonstrate a number of qualities personal to her. She notes those down and then develops the list by adding a number of additional things she is proud of because they show situations where she has persisted and overcome challenges. The result is a list of affirmations that are personal to her:

Joanna's affirmations:

- I brought up my two children as well as I could.

- I am a good listener.

- I usually try my best at things, even if I don't always succeed.

- I am kind-hearted.

- Despite having a difficult background I managed to gain professional qualifications as a lawyer.

- I recognize my limitations.

- I have made efforts to start my life again after difficult times.

- I have a sense of humour.

- I have grown onions in my garden.

- I am a good cook – particularly of Spanish food.

- I am naturally shy but have made efforts to talk to people.

- I am loyal to my friends.

- I had the courage to get out of a difficult relationship.

As you can see from the above list, you can put virtually anything down as an achievement or ability – the important thing is that it is something you have done or an aspect of your personality that is *meaningful to you and you are proud of it.*

THE VALUE OF AFFIRMATIONS

You may have noticed that I called Joanna's personal statements 'affirmations'.

---

key term

An **affirmation** in this context is a positive statement about a quality or achievement that you can lay claim to.

The value of affirmations is that they help you to build a sense of positive personal identity in a way that is unique to you. If created in a sensible way they can help you to deal with negative thoughts about yourself, give appropriate acknowledgement to things that you are proud of and raise your self-esteem. However, there are some important features that it is important to remember when you try to create affirmations for yourself, which are indicated in the paragraphs that follow.

Once you have created a list of affirmations personal to you, keep it to hand and read it regularly at first, and subsequently at any time when you are feeling negative about yourself, to help you retrain your mind into recognizing positive features about yourself and your life.

CHARACTERISTICS OF HELPFUL AFFIRMATIONS

Keep affirmations realistic: You may sometimes come across the idea of using very general affirmations about yourself such as 'I am a wonderful person' or 'I can achieve whatever I want.' I would advise against this on the basis that if you do this you are lurching from one extreme to another. Is it really true that you can achieve whatever you want? Probably not – it might be if what you want is limited to things that are within your sole control but normally people want some things that are not completely within their control, so you need to be realistic otherwise you will create an affirmation which just sounds hollow and is unlikely to be fulfilled.

Similarly, if you tend to have negative thoughts such as 'I always make a mess of things', having an affirmation to counter this which says: 'I *never* make a mess of things' or 'I *always* make the right choices' would be ludicrous. It would be better to counter the global negative thought which the more realistic thought: 'I *sometimes* make the right choice' or even 'I don't *always* make a mess of things', which although it's not sensational is at least realistic and an improvement on the original negative thought.

Make your affirmations specific: Sometimes in the helping professions a distinction is also drawn between making generalized comments about a person, which puts them in a box and can be inaccurate, unhelpful or offensive, and the alternative of giving focused specific comments on a person's actions or behaviour, which can be useful. If someone does something that you think is undesirable it is usually more helpful to indicate that you don't agree with their specific action (and say why) rather than to label them generally in negative terms. Similarly, if someone does something you think is *good*, you can often provide the most helpful feedback by highlighting and praising their *specific positive action* rather than by generalized praise. The same principle applies to your own comments about yourself: I would suggest that with your affirmations you focus on specific behaviours that you sometimes show, positive actions that you have done, or characteristics that you have which you are proud of, rather than on giving vague positive labels which are likely to be unconvincing and/or exaggerated – 'I have completed a marathon' (if it is true) is more helpful than 'I am a great runner', which is likely to be an exaggeration or a generalized value judgement at best.

Express affirmations in the first person: It also tends to be helpful if affirmations are expressed in the first person e.g. 'I have …' or 'I am …'. There are two main reasons for this:

1. Valuing yourself is not about matching up to a perceived standard set by others or by society. It is the very opposite – it is about *you* taking responsibility for *your life* and *your decisions*, so it is a good idea for you to take ownership of what you value in yourself as part of this process.

2. Using the 'I' form helps to reinforce the fact that you are acknowledging and recognizing your own personal identity in a constructive way, not dismissing yourself or disregarding yourself – this is all part of valuing yourself.

REMEMBER

Personal affirmations are more likely to be helpful in building your self-esteem in a lasting way if they:

- Are realistic, not exaggerated

- Can be evidenced or demonstrated by examples

- Are specific, referring to particular actions, achievements or attributes rather than applying a general rating to yourself as a human being

- Are expressed in the first person.

try it now

Use the space below to create your own list of qualities, abilities and achievements. Write out next to the bullet points a list of anything that you are proud of having achieved or that you see as an ability or quality in yourself. This list is personal to you. It's about what you personally are proud of, irrespective of what others might think. Use the first person to introduce each item, e.g. 'I have ...' or 'I am ...'.

Personal affirmations:

- ....

- ....

- ....

- ....

- ....

- ....

- ....

- ....

- ....

- ....

DO'S AND DON'TS OF AFFIRMATIONS

The purpose of affirmations is to help you value yourself in a realistic way and to counter a negative self-image or exaggerated negative thoughts about yourself.

If you suffer from low self-esteem then the negative picture of yourself and the negative thoughts about yourself are likely to be automatic and may well have been going on for a long time (in some cases from before you can remember). They can be changed or modified but this takes some conscious effort and practice, so you need to find ways of keeping your affirmations in your consciousness. Thus I suggest you consider the following do's and don'ts:

Do's: To help keep your personal affirmations in your consciousness, try any or all of the following:

- Read through them on a daily basis.

- Keep copies where you will see them, for example on the fridge door or the dashboard of your car.

- Keep a copy in a diary or a purse or wallet for reference when needed.

Don'ts: There is one main 'don't' in relation to personal affirmations:

- *Don't stick your affirmations list in a drawer and forget about it once you've compiled it.*

WHAT TO DO IF YOU HAVE TROUBLE CREATING AFFIRMATIONS

Some people have difficulty thinking of anything positive to say about themselves or are reluctant to do so. If you find it difficult to produce a list of affirmations, you can ask yourself the following questions (and write down your answers) to get some ideas of things that you can be proud of to include in your affirmations list:

- What would a close friend say were my *qualities*? (If not sure, then ask them.)

- What would a close friend say were my *abilities and achievements*? (Again, if not sure, ask them.)

- What challenges have I faced in my life? Give a positive statement of what you have done when faced with them. (Even if you don't feel you have fully overcome them, give yourself credit for what you have tried to do.)

- What characteristics annoy me in other people which I do *not* have? Create a positive statement out of the opposite – e.g. if you are not cruel, reframe that as 'I can be kind' or 'I am caring' or a similar expression that seems accurate to you.

- What changes have I made in my life (however small) of which I am proud?

- What skills have I learned? (This might be through training, at school or college, or in a job, or from others such as family or friends.)

- How would someone who thinks well of me describe me?

VALIDATING YOUR AFFIRMATIONS

I mentioned that affirmations tend to be more helpful in building your self-esteem if they can be evidenced or demonstrated. If you write a personal affirmation down and it doesn't seem real to you then write down the arguments or evidence that support it. Reminding yourself of them can help to remind you that the affirmation is valid and is not just a wild claim!

case study
JAMES: GIVING YOUR AFFIRMATIONS CREDIBILITY

James is in his early thirties, working in a professional role for a large company. He is well respected in his work but keeps comparing himself to others professionally and worrying that he isn't doing as well as he should. In his personal life he has a number of positive relationships but in his own mind he thinks of himself as unlikeable and boring. He creates a list of affirmations but finds that some of them seem hollow to him, so to help him recognize that he is not just imagining these positives he selects the ones he is doubtful about and validates them by writing down evidence to support each one, as indicated below:

Affirmation: I am fair-minded.
Illustration or supporting evidence: Tim complimented me for helping him to see different views in an argument he was having with a friend and others have said that they think I am a good judge of character and of situations.

Affirmation: I am competent in my job.
Illustration or supporting evidence: My performance reviews have been positive.

Affirmation: I can be fun.
Illustration or supporting evidence: Gary, Fiona, Carol and I had a laugh at the ice rink on Saturday.

If you have difficulty in believing the affirmations you write about yourself then try doing a similar exercise, writing down the supporting evidence for any of the affirmations you are having difficulty with.

ACKNOWLEDGING POSITIVE ACTIONS, CHARACTERISTICS AND ACTIVITIES

People who have a reasonable level of self-esteem can see positives in their actions. This doesn't mean that they necessarily brag about it but they are comfortable with the way they act. They may realistically and sensibly examine whether they could have done something differently or better, but they do not continually doubt themselves or their actions.

People with low self-esteem tend to take the opposite view of their actions. If you have low self-esteem you are likely to find it difficult to see positives in your actions. To redress the balance usually requires some conscious effort.

try it now

For a week from now keep a Positives Diary (see the form opposite), identifying what you have done in the day and any positive characteristics you have shown. For the purposes of this exercise, just record the positives in the day, however small or few in number, and even if they only seem like small or easy things to you. If this works well for you, continue it for the following week. Once you have kept your Positives Diary for a week or two, see if there is anything from it that you can adapt to add to your list of personal affirmations.

Note: If you try keeping a Positives Diary but are unable to find *anything* that you recognize as a personal achievement or something you enjoyed doing, then it is possible that you are experiencing depression. If you think that might be the case, then speak to your doctor to check out whether that is so and to get appropriate support.

LIMITING BELIEFS

So far in this chapter I have focused primarily on positive actions and exercises that you can follow if you have an overly negative self-image, to help build a realistic and positive impression of yourself.

The complementary approach, which it is likely to be helpful for you to adopt if you don't value yourself, is to tackle directly the underlying beliefs that are making it hard for you to see yourself positively or realistically. Those underlying beliefs may be limiting your capacity to develop your potential.

POSITIVES DIARY: WEEK COMMENCING

	Things I achieved (however small)	Things I enjoyed (however silly)	Positive characteristics I showed
Monday			
Tuesday			
Wednesday			
Thursday			
Friday			
Saturday			
Sunday			

There are a number of different types of limiting belief. Here are some examples:

- **Limiting beliefs about your abilities:** 'I am never any good at anything.'

- **Limiting beliefs about your personality or characteristics:** 'I am stupid' or 'I am over emotional' or, by contrast, 'I am cold-hearted.'

- **Limiting beliefs about how you ought to act:** 'It's wrong to put yourself first' or 'You shouldn't argue.'

- **Limiting beliefs about the consequences of acting in a certain way:** 'If I say I disagree with them, they will dislike me' or 'If I get close to him/her, he/she will leave me.'

- **Limiting beliefs about particular groups of people:** 'Men are afraid of commitment' or 'Women are manipulative.'

- **Limiting beliefs about the world in general or life:** 'Good things never last' or 'Everyone is out to get what they want for themselves.'

Some of the points in a limiting belief may *sometimes* be true or an accurate description of a particular instance or a particular person, but once the belief is set out as a hard and fast rule, rather than a specific observation or an idea which you are aiming to test in an objective way, then it can lead you to make assumptions about situations which are not accurate, or perhaps even worse, it can lead you to miss out on an opportunity to have a positive experience or positive relationship.

In terms of your own well-being and self-esteem, if you apply a rigid, demanding expectation of how you feel you should be, then you may well be too hard on yourself if you don't quite match up to the standard of perfection you have set for yourself.

USEFUL TIP

Watch out for thoughts you have or statements you make that are generalizations or prescriptions for how you or other people should live or be, such as 'I must ...' or 'I ought to ...' or 'they should ...' or 'they shouldn't ...'. Thoughts like these may sometimes help to guide your life but if you adhere to them too rigidly or inflexibly you may find yourself being very judgemental about other people or about yourself.

One of the most famous examples of a limiting belief is the belief held by many people prior to 6 May 1954 that it was impossible for a human being to run a mile in under four minutes.

What happened on 6 May 1954? Roger Bannister ran a four-minute mile.

That opened the floodgates. Suddenly other athletes realized that it *was* possible to run a mile in under four minutes and were no longer held back by the conscious or unconscious limiting belief that it was not possible. Within three years, sixteen runners had broken the four-minute mile. This contrasted with a nine-year period before Bannister's run in which no one had been able to improve on the old record of 4 minutes 1.4 seconds.

This one example shows what a powerful difference it can make if someone – in this case, Roger Bannister – is able to overcome a limiting belief that has held them and others back.

THE IMPACT OF LIMITING BELIEFS ABOUT YOURSELF

If you have negative limiting beliefs about your own characteristics or capabilities then these are likely to contribute to and reinforce your own lack of self-esteem.

For example, if you believe that you do not deserve to be happy then you may well not put yourself into situations where you might become happy or where you might have an opportunity to do something or get something that you would like.

In this kind of situation, your limiting beliefs are leading to unhelpful actions with predictable negative results that then reinforce your limiting belief. This can be expressed in a flow chart:

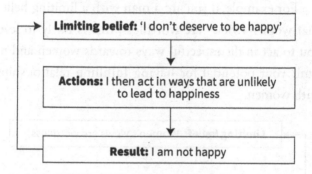

If you believe that you are stupid then you may well not put yourself into situations where you could learn and gain knowledge because you fear failure or you fear that others may come to the same negative view about your abilities that you have.

If you believe that you are over-emotional then you may well not challenge yourself to act in calm ways because you have an internal script in your head telling you that this is a feature of yourself that you cannot change (even if it isn't).

THE IMPACT OF LIMITING BELIEFS INVOLVING OTHER PEOPLE

Limiting beliefs about other people or their behaviour towards you, and what it means, or limiting beliefs about the world in general, can also impact adversely on your self-esteem. This may sometimes be in an indirect way so that you do not always realize it.

For example, if you are a man with a limiting belief that women's views are worthless, this is likely to lead you to act in disrespectful ways towards women and to limit your potential for having fulfilling relationships with women.

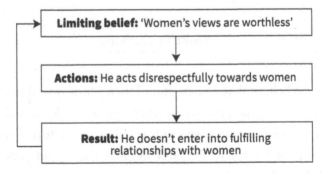

Alternatively, if you are a woman with a limiting belief that men are always selfish, then this may lead you to act in disrespectful, dismissive or suspicious ways towards men, with equally problematic results.

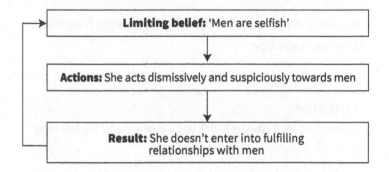

Limiting belief: 'Men are selfish'

Actions: She acts dismissively and suspiciously towards men

Result: She doesn't enter into fulfilling relationships with men

The above examples focus on hypothetical limiting beliefs held by a man about women or by a woman about men. Of course, limiting beliefs can be held by women about women or men about men too, and they can be held by any individuals whatever their sexual orientation. They are not just the prerogative of one group of people or one section of society!

It is important to identify your limiting beliefs about others and what their behaviour means as well as those you hold about yourself.

IDENTIFYING YOUR LIMITING BELIEFS

If you are already aware of some of your limiting beliefs, don't beat yourself up about it. It is much more usual to have some than to have none at all and the fact that you are already aware of some suggests a degree of self-awareness. If you want to identify your limiting beliefs, or to clarify them or find others that you might have, then here are some tips:

IDENTIFYING LIMITING BELIEFS THROUGH YOUR INNER CONVERSATIONS

Most people (and I include myself) have an inner conversation going on in their head when they think about their interactions with others, events or situations they are involved in or may enter into, and their day-to-day lives and responsibilities. This is likely to be a commentary on your own fears or hopes about what is happening or likely to happen.

One way to identify limiting beliefs is to become aware of your inner conversations and in particular of any self-critical thoughts that you have. Look for any patterns and reflect on whether behind a particular self-critical thought there might be a general limiting belief that you have about yourself or the world, which leads you to move to the self-critical or negative thought quicker than some others might.

try it now

Think back to a particular situation recently when you were self-critical and unhappy about the way you acted. If possible, choose a situation where your self-critical thoughts were the kind of thoughts that you have quite a lot. Write down the headings listed in the example below, then note down your responses: describe briefly what the situation was and what your self-critical thoughts were; then reflect on whether there might have been a limiting belief underlying the thought; finally, give any reasons why having that limiting belief may be unhelpful. An example is given to start you off:

Situation: Taking my driving test
Self-critical thought(s): 'I haven't a chance of passing the test.'
Underlying limiting belief: 'I never achieve what I want.'
How is the limiting belief unhelpful? It leads me to be anxious or demotivated, which limits my chances of achieving what I want to and leads me to feel bad.

Note: In doing this exercise be sure to write down limiting beliefs that apply to you – don't just put down what you think other people might say were limiting beliefs – this is about establishing what *you* think is limiting you. If you think that there may be more than one limiting belief behind a particular thought then you can put them all down and reflect on the consequences of each in turn.

USEFUL TIP

If your self-critical thought is a negative prediction about yourself, as in the example above, or an instruction to yourself that you should or should not do something, then ask yourself *why* you think you won't achieve what you want (in the above instance) or *why* you should not act in a particular way. That may help you to clarify what the underlying limiting beliefs are.

THE DOWNWARD ARROW TECHNIQUE

If you have difficulty identifying your limiting beliefs then one technique that can help you to do so is the downward arrow technique (also known as the vertical arrow technique).

To use this technique, you take a negative or anxious thought that you are thinking and then ask yourself 'What does that mean?' or 'What does that show?' Whatever answer you give, apply the same question to it, and keep doing that with each answer you give, until you reach a point which you feel reflects the limiting belief that underlies the thought.

You can also use other variations for the question that you use, depending on the context, such as 'So what?' or 'What's so bad about that?' or 'Why does that matter?' or 'What does that say about me?' The aim is to clarify why you feel so strongly about the situation.

USEFUL TIP

To help find your limiting beliefs, try applying the downward arrow technique to a situation where you feel strongly negative about yourself or about something you have or haven't achieved – strong negative emotion about yourself can be an indicator that there may be a limiting belief involved.

case study

EAMONN: USING THE DOWNWARD ARROW TECHNIQUE

Eamonn is going to attend a job interview but the train he is on is delayed and he arrives late. He doesn't get the job. He feels very down and thinks: 'It was just my luck to get a train that was delayed.'

Eamonn then uses the downward arrow technique to find out if there are limiting beliefs involved:

   Q: 'What does that show?'
   A: 'Whenever I seem to have an opportunity it disappears'
   Q: 'What does that show?'
   A: 'I'm never going to succeed' (limiting belief)

Q: 'What does that show?'
A: 'I'm useless' (limiting belief)

Of course, different people using the downward arrow technique may find that they have different limiting beliefs to Eamonn's in a similar situation. Someone else might reach the answer that this situation shows that 'The world is against me', which would be a different type of limiting belief from the one Eamonn has. To determine what your own limiting beliefs are you need to do the exercise for yourself.

try it now

Think back to a situation where you felt strongly negative about yourself and use the downward arrow technique to try to establish if there are any limiting beliefs involved, and if so, what they might be.

LIMITING BELIEFS INVOLVING RELATIONSHIPS

Relationships are an area where many people have limiting beliefs about themselves or others that impact on their self-esteem and their ability to value themselves. You can use a similar method to that above specifically to identify limiting beliefs involving relationships if you think this is an area of particular relevance to you.

case study LOUISE: ADDRESSING LIMITING BELIEFS ABOUT RELATIONSHIPS

Louise is doubtful of her ability to have a successful romantic relationship with a man. When she enters into a relationship she has a tendency to get very anxious at any sign that might be interpreted as a lack of interest from her partner. Using a series of headings similar to those set out previously on page 43, but adapted specifically to observe anxious thoughts in relationships, she analyzes a situation in which Simon, her partner of six months, didn't ring her one evening when he had said he would – behaviour which is untypical for him:

Situation: Simon didn't ring me.

Thought (about others): He is deliberately not ringing me because he is not interested in seeing me. He would prefer to do something else.

Underlying limiting belief(s):
(a) I am unattractive.
(b) Men don't like commitment.

How are the limiting beliefs unhelpful?
- They discourage me from checking whether there are other explanations for Simon not ringing me.

- They lead me to feel bad about myself and see myself as a victim.

- The first belief makes it hard for me to act confidently in relationships with men and the second belief makes it hard for me to develop a trusting relationship with a man.

CHANGING LIMITING BELIEFS

Once you have identified your limiting beliefs, the next step is to explore whether you want to try to change some of them. Since they are likely to be deeply held beliefs or prejudices, questioning them requires some effort. Here is a checklist of questions that you can use to explore what it might be like if you opened yourself to the possibility of a slightly different view:

1. What would be a less extreme belief (or beliefs) that I might hold?

2. What would be the advantages for me of holding the new belief(s) rather than the limiting belief(s)?

3. What would be the potential disadvantages for me of holding the new belief(s) instead of the old one(s)?

case study LOUISE (CONTINUED): EXPLORING ALTERNATIVES TO LIMITING BELIEFS

Louise asks herself the questions in the checklist and comes up with the following answers:

1. *What would be less extreme beliefs that I might hold?*
- 'Some men find me attractive and some don't.'
- 'Some men don't want commitment in a relationship but others do.'

2. *What would be the advantages for me of holding the new beliefs rather than the limiting beliefs?*
- I would be more likely to discuss the situation with Simon in a positive way.
- I would have a greater chance of building trust in a relationship with a man.
- I would feel more optimistic about the possibility of a lasting relationship with a man.
- I would feel more able to open up about my own insecurities without prejudging the result.

3. *What would be the potential disadvantages for me of holding the new beliefs instead of the old ones?*
- I might make an idiot of myself.
- I might get hurt.
- I would have to give up a long-standing belief!
- It would mean that it was partly my fault that I haven't developed a more long-term relationship before.
- If the belief is true it would be foolish to give it up!

ADOPTING AN EXPERIMENTAL ATTITUDE

Louise's answers to the three questions in the checklist indicate that there could be significant benefits for her if she can start to hold less extreme beliefs but also that there are significant disadvantages for her in doing so. If you find yourself caught in a similar kind of dilemma about whether a less extreme belief might be more helpful to you than a particular limiting belief that you hold, then you can do the following to help you get to a stage where you are willing to test out the alternative belief:

1. Remind yourself that what you are going to do is to try *acting as if* the alternative, more moderate, belief might be true *as an experiment* but that doesn't commit you to believing it.

2. Try to find a way of testing out the alternative belief that will not make it difficult to cope if your experiment doesn't work out. One thing that you can do in this respect is to think of constructive things that you can do or say to yourself if the experiment doesn't work out – in the next chapter I will be looking at the idea of 'balancing thoughts' (see pages 74–81). These can be particularly helpful for dealing with situations you are anxious about.

3. When you assess the results of your experiment, note down any positive consequences of your new way of acting and any negative consequences. Bear in mind that because you have long held the limiting belief you may be tempted to view results in a negative way rather than to notice the positives so try not to jump to conclusions too quickly.

You can use a series of headings like the ones given below (set out as a list or in a table) to note down the results of your experimentation with alternative beliefs:

Initial situation and thoughts:
Initial limiting belief:
Alternative belief:
Actions I tried in line with alternative belief:
Result:

case study LOUISE (CONTINUED): RECORDING THE RESULTS OF AN EXPERIMENT

After thinking through her answers to the questions, Louise decides that although she feels convinced of her judgement about men not liking commitment and also finds it hard to believe that she might be considered attractive, she is going to act *as if* the possible alternatives ('Some men find me attractive and some don't'; 'Some men don't want commitment in a relationship but others do') might be true in this instance. She decides to begin by discussing the situation with Simon in a non-confrontational way while also explaining some of her own feelings of insecurity around it. She does so and keeps a record of the results:

Initial situation and thoughts: Simon didn't ring me. I thought 'He is not interested in seeing me.'

Initial limiting belief:
(a) 'I am unattractive.'
(b) 'Men don't like commitment.'

Alternative belief:

(a) 'Some men find me attractive and some don't.'

(b) 'Some men don't want commitment in a relationship but others do.'

Actions I tried in line with alternative belief: I checked with Simon why he didn't ring me and also explained in a non-aggressive way some of my insecure feelings.

Result: Simon said he had been involved in finishing some decorating in his house and by the time he looked at his watch it was too late to ring.

We discussed some of my feelings of insecurity and he reassured me that he did find me attractive. We had an interesting discussion about the issue of commitment. I'm not quite sure where that takes us but I feel better for at least having had the discussion!

The results of Louise's experiment didn't in one go create a fulfilling relationship for her but they *were* the first step in opening up a dialogue. The next chapter – on *accepting yourself* – will give further ideas which can help you to deal with negative thought patterns that can be relevant to low self-esteem. In chapter 4 on *understanding yourself*, I will also explore the question of where your negative beliefs about yourself may have come from and give some further ideas for what you can do about them.

While you are working on these things you can also begin to consider the second element of the VALUE acronym, *accepting yourself*, which forms the subject matter of chapter 2.

CHAPTER 2

Accept yourself

'Grant me the serenity to accept what I can't
change, the courage to change what I can
and the wisdom to know the difference.'
—Reinhold Niebuhr

DEVELOPING AN ATTITUDE OF SELF-ACCEPTANCE

Self-acceptance means valuing yourself even if you do not achieve everything you want or do not always act in the way you think you should. The most lasting kind of self-acceptance involves recognizing that you can make mistakes and have flaws in your character without that meaning that you are worthless.

CONDITIONAL AND UNCONDITIONAL SELF-ACCEPTANCE

In his book *The Myth of Self-Esteem* (2005), the psychologist Albert Ellis distinguished between **conditional self-acceptance,** where your feelings about your self-worth are dependent on achieving some kind of goal (for example success in work or the approval of others) and

unconditional self-acceptance, where you value yourself irrespective of whether you achieve goals or obtain the respect of others.

Ellis advocated unconditional self-acceptance. He acknowledged that conditional self-acceptance can result in benefits – placing a high importance on achieving personal goals or cultivating relationships can *sometimes* motivate you to achieve more. However, he saw it as having serious drawbacks:

- It can lead you to feel very bad about yourself if you don't achieve important goals.

- It can lead you to focus too much on superficial achievements.

- It may incline you to be dishonest (because you don't want to admit to failure) or to seek social approval rather than to act with integrity.

Ellis (in *The Myth of Self-Esteem*) and others such as David Burns (in his book *Ten Days to Self-Esteem*) argue forcefully that unconditional self-acceptance and having a healthy view of yourself is linked to not rating yourself *globally* as worthless or inferior. If you can accept yourself for what you are and see yourself as having an intrinsic worth whether or not you achieve particular personal goals or gain compliments from other people then this can help you to be less vulnerable to low self-esteem.

In Ellis's view it is okay to rate *your success in relation to* particular goals or aspirations but try to avoid judging yourself generally, or your overall worth, on the basis of whether you do or don't succeed in a particular task or goal.

try it now

Each time you catch yourself being self-critical or you do not achieve a goal, acknowledge to yourself that you have not achieved your goal or that you wish that you had acted differently but then remind yourself that it does *not* mean that you are worthless. If it helps, when you do this you can also remind yourself of the affirmations that you created in chapter 1 (page 28).

BENEFITS OF ACCEPTING YOURSELF UNCONDITIONALLY

There are a number of potential benefits that can ensue if you accept yourself unconditionally. If you regard yourself as having worth irrespective of whether or not you achieve particular goals, act in certain ways or gain the approval of others, then:

- You may feel happier, because you do not feel so much pressure to achieve or to be a certain way.

- You are unlikely to get so despondent if you fail to achieve a particular goal.

- You may well be better able to make decisions for yourself because you do not feel that your worth is reliant on the opinions of other people.

- You do not experience the stress of frequently comparing yourself to other people or to excessively high standards.

DISADVANTAGES OF ACCEPTING YOURSELF UNCONDITIONALLY

There may however be some potential disadvantages from accepting yourself unconditionally, such as:

- You may lose some of your drive because you feel you don't have to prove yourself so much.

- You may become lazier.

- You may become inconsiderate or disrespectful of others if you go to the extreme of not valuing the opinion of others at all or of thinking that you are completely self-sufficient.

You can minimize the likelihood of the disadvantages arising if you remember that your aim, as suggested at the beginning of chapter 1 (page 11), is not to have a super-high level of self-esteem (which might involve arrogance or conceit) but merely to achieve a *reasonable* level of self-esteem. Accepting yourself unconditionally does not have to mean that you become arrogant. Indeed Albert Ellis advocated in many of his books that alongside aiming for unconditional self-acceptance, you should also try to aim for unconditional acceptance of others – the two aims can be complementary.

try it now

Write a list of what the benefits and disadvantages might be *for you* if you were able to move closer towards an attitude of unconditional self-acceptance. Do the benefits outweigh the disadvantages? Is there any way that you can minimize the risk of the disadvantages you have identified occurring, or else manage them if they do occur?

NOT JUDGING YOURSELF

Linked to the idea of unconditional self-acceptance is the idea of not judging yourself for your perceived weaknesses or failings. One way that you can help to do this is by keeping a conscious record of your internal descriptions of your own perceived failings and errors, then *reframing* the negative descriptive language in which you originally described the failings in a less emotionally charged, more specific and neutral way, so that you are not making a moral judgement on yourself.

case study MARCIA: REFRAMING NEGATIVE JUDGEMENTS ABOUT YOURSELF

Marcia's relationship with her partner of two years has just ended and she has become very self-critical, questioning whether the end of the relationship was due to some personal failing of hers. To help herself adopt a more accepting stance towards herself she makes a note of the language with which she criticizes herself and then in her mind reframes the descriptions, taking out the more judgemental phrases in them, so that they are more neutral and less emotionally charged:

Negative self-description: 'I am disgustingly fat.'
Reframed neutral description: 'I have difficulty controlling my weight and do not have the body shape that I would like.'

Negative self-description: 'I am very poor at telling people my real feelings.'
Reframed neutral description: 'I don't express my feelings to others as much as I would like to.'

Negative self-description: 'I am uselessly disorganized.'
Reframed neutral description: 'I don't organize my work tasks as efficiently as some people.'

Negative self-description: 'I am hopeless at relationships.'
Reframed neutral description: 'I am not currently in a relationship.'

CHANGING PRESCRIPTIONS INTO PREFERENCES

Another technique recommended by Albert Ellis that you can use to help you accept both yourself and others is this: every time you catch yourself making a prescriptive statement about how you or someone else *should be* or *should behave*, such as 'I must ...' or 'I ought to ...', reframe that statement in your mind (or indeed out loud if you are speaking to someone) so that you express a personal preference, wish, hope or intention rather than an inflexible prescription. For example, instead of 'I mustn't slip up this time' say to yourself 'I am going to try not to slip up this time' or 'I hope that I don't slip up this time.' This may help to reduce your tension and stress and in doing so it may actually also increase your chances of success.

ACCEPTING YOUR PHYSICAL APPEARANCE

If some of your negative feelings about yourself relate to your appearance, then you can try an exercise involving looking in a full-length mirror and honestly focusing on each of the 'bad' aspects of your body that you dislike, but trying to do so in a detached observational way rather than in an emotional self-condemnatory way. Nathaniel Branden in his book *The Six Pillars of Self-Esteem* and Ellis in *The Myth of Self-Esteem* both include an exercise of this type in order to help with self-acceptance around body image (Ellis attributes the version he describes to Jeffrey Brandsma).

The crucial element in doing this exercise of scrutinizing your physical imperfections is to try to do it with an attitude of calmness and acceptance (difficult as that is). Acceptance here doesn't mean that you say you are not going to try to do anything to improve aspects of yourself that you don't like or that you are not going to try to become healthier but it does mean that *if you don't succeed in changing yourself you still accept yourself.* You can focus on aspects that you want to change and work out a plan to try to do that but at the same time remind yourself that you can accept those perceived imperfections and continue to act and live in positive ways whether or not you achieve your desired change.

For some people, learning not to judge yourself or your physical appearance too harshly can be extremely difficult. In these circumstances, you may find it helps to use *detached self-observation* to note your thoughts, feelings and sensations when you are being judgemental about yourself.

USEFUL TIP

When you have a negative thought about yourself or your appearance, try simply to *observe* your thoughts and feelings and sensations or physiological changes in a detached way. To help you with this detached observation, you may find it useful to describe your thoughts/feelings/sensations in the third person (as illustrated in the example below). When doing so, imagine you are a friendly third party observing yourself in a compassionate way, or alternatively imagine you are a scientist observing yourself in a detached way as if you were reporting data.

For example, someone trying the exercise of looking in the mirror and scrutinizing their body might report his thoughts, feelings etc. to himself thus (using the third person rather than 'I'): 'John is looking at his stomach, John is thinking he is fat, John is upset, John is feeling tense, John is trying to relax his shoulders ...'.

As in the above example, if you use this detached reporting technique and you still find negative feelings intruding, try not to be critical of yourself for having them, just report them and then move on to your next observation if you can.

You may also find that meditation and breathing techniques can help you achieve the kind of calmness and detachment that can help with accepting yourself. Chapter 4 on *understanding yourself* contains further information about basic meditation practice (pages 160–2).

A HEALTHY ATTITUDE TOWARDS YOUR OWN FAULTS OR FAILINGS

Below are set out *three different attitudes* that you might have when reflecting on your own faults:

1. Defensiveness/denial: You don't admit to yourself that you have the faults or you minimize them because you see them as shameful, bad or even unforgiveable.

2. Acceptance (without judging yourself): You acknowledge failings, faults and errors honestly and accept yourself at the same time, realizing that everybody has faults.

3. Self-condemnation: You see your faults and condemn yourself as a human being for having them, not recognizing that it is normal to have faults and make mistakes or fail in some enterprises.

Consistent with Ellis's ideas on unconditional self-acceptance, I would suggest that the middle category – acceptance of your faults or failings without judging yourself – is a sounder basis for a reasonable level of self-esteem than either of the two extremes.

THE ABC MODEL OF EMOTIONS

Some time before writing his book on self-esteem, Ellis developed a famous model for looking at the relationship between thought patterns and emotions, which can also be usefully applied to helping you deal with issues around self-acceptance. In its initial formulation this model was called the 'ABC model of emotions'. It has come to be one of the most famous methods used in cognitive behavioural therapy (or CBT). The model analyzes the development of emotions in the sequence **A:** activating event; **B:** belief; **C:** consequent emotion. (In some of his books Ellis uses the phrase 'adversity' in place of 'activating event' because the context in which CBT is used is often one where the initial activating event is something which appears to the person on the receiving end of it to be an adverse or problematic situation.)

A simple example of an analysis using the ABC model of emotions would be:

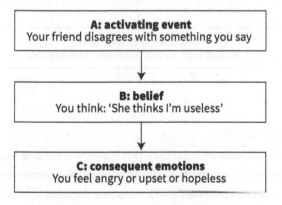

A: activating event
Your friend disagrees with something you say

B: belief
You think: 'She thinks I'm useless'

C: consequent emotions
You feel angry or upset or hopeless

In this example you may well be regarding yourself in a non-accepting way – jumping from the mere fact that your friend disagrees with you to the belief that she must be thinking you are useless, and seeing that as awful.

Another example of using the ABC model to analyze a situation in which you don't adopt an accepting attitude towards yourself and your actions is given below:

A: activating event
I forgot to include one of the papers that I was supposed
to bring to a meeting and I found it difficult
to contribute to the discussion about the topic

B: belief
'Why can't I ever do what I intend to? I am so disorganized.
My work colleague would never have done this. I am stupid.'

C: consequent emotions
Annoyed with myself, frustrated and stressed

---

try it now

When you have an experience that leaves you passing negative
judgements on yourself, use Ellis's ABC model to record the activating event that prompted your feelings; the thoughts or beliefs that
went through your mind; and your consequent emotions. (Next we
will start to consider what you might do to address these negative,
self-critical judgements!)

DISPUTING WITH YOURSELF – A ROUTE TO GREATER SELF-ACCEPTANCE

Ellis later added onto his ABC model a 'D' standing for 'disputation' (and also an 'E' to stand for the positive 'effects' of this disputation, or the 'energizing' results of it). The 'D' for 'disputation' gives the key to what is likely to be helpful for you if you want to break a pattern of self-critical thoughts and negative feelings about yourself – namely using techniques to dispute and challenge your own self-critical thinking.

It may sound strange to suggest that disputing with yourself might lead you to accept yourself more. However, the idea is to dispute irrational, overly negative and self-critical thoughts, so that your thinking becomes more *balanced*. Here is a **disputation checklist** of key questions I suggest you use to help you do this:

1. Ask yourself: 'If I were talking to a friend who was in my situation and they were expressing those self-critical thoughts, what would I say to them?'
   The response might include suggestions like:
   – 'Don't be so hard on yourself.'
   – 'No one else noticed so it didn't really matter.'

2. Alternatively, imagine a reasonable and supportive friend is talking to you about your self-critical perception of yourself. What might they say to you?

This might include similar things to the above, or other points specifically related to the situation or to your personal qualities, such as:

- 'Maybe organization is not your strong point but you've got other more important qualities, like being a good friend.'
- 'It isn't the most important situation. You made a mistake, that's all. We all do it from time to time.'

3. Ask yourself if your self-critical assessment is *accurate* or *exaggerated* – for example, if you find that your self-critical statement includes the words 'never' or 'always' you may be able to soften it by recognizing that *sometimes* you make the mistake or act in the way you feel bad about, but *on other occasions* you do act in the positive way that you would like.

4. Ask yourself if there any similar occasions when you have acted positively. Often people remember mistakes and failures but not successes, so to put the situation into context, acknowledge that *on this occasion* you perhaps didn't act as you would have liked but remind yourself that *on other occasions* you have done so.

5. Even if your self-critical thought is true, ask yourself how much it really matters? Is it really as important

as you think? Is it a matter of life and death or just something that in an ideal world you might have done differently?

Once you have gone through the checklist, create a sentence based on one or more of your answers. Say that sentence to yourself when experiencing the self-critical thoughts, so as to challenge them and put them in a more balanced perspective (we will look in greater detail at this idea of creating a 'balancing thought' or 'balancing statement' later in this chapter – see pages 74–81).

REMEMBER

In a situation that you have analyzed using the ABC model, or in another situation where you are being highly critical of yourself, remember the 'D' for 'disputation' and try to challenge your self-critical thoughts by asking yourself the five questions in the disputation checklist above.

CBT AND SELF-ACCEPTANCE

Ellis was one of two people who in the second half of the twentieth century came up with related though not identical ideas that later came to be described under the umbrella term 'cognitive behavioural therapy', or CBT for short. His approach was influenced by the thinking of ancient Greek philosophers such as Epictetus, who held that 'Men are disturbed not by things, but by the view which they take of them.'

Cognitive behavioural therapy builds on the idea in the above quote by encouraging you to try to look at situations, problems and relationships in fresh or different ways, and to take responsibility for the way in which you look at and react to events. Ellis's approach, which he first began to use in the mid-1950s and developed over subsequent decades, enabled clients to change self-defeating beliefs by helping them to see the irrationality or inflexibility inherent in those beliefs. Ellis called his approach rational therapy (later renamed 'rational emotive therapy' or 'rational emotive behaviour therapy'). As indicated above, it is also often seen as a form of cognitive behavioural therapy.

The other key figure in the development of CBT theories is Dr Aaron Beck. Beck developed his system of 'cognitive therapy' in the early 1960s as a psychiatrist at the University of Pennsylvania. He had studied and practised psychoanalysis and in order to seek research validation for the theories of psychoanalysis he conducted research to test psychoanalytic concepts of depression. To his surprise he found that the research results did *not* validate the psychoanalytic concepts so he started to test and research alternative methods. The ideas that he developed, like Ellis's, can be used to help you deal with issues of low self-esteem and to develop greater self-acceptance if you have a tendency to dismiss and belittle yourself and your efforts.

NEGATIVE AUTOMATIC THOUGHTS

Working with patients who were depressed, Beck found that rather than the psychoanalytic concepts that he had been expecting to discover, a frequent thread in the depressed patients was that they often experienced negative thoughts which appeared to occur spontaneously, for which he coined the term 'automatic thoughts'. The patients' thoughts fell into three types:

1. Negative thoughts about yourself

2. Negative thoughts about the world

3. Negative thoughts about the future.

The first type of negative thoughts, thoughts about yourself, are highly relevant to the topic of self-esteem and in particular to self-acceptance. Everyone has *some* negative thoughts about their self but if you *often* have negative thoughts about yourself and the things that you do or don't do, or if your negative thoughts are extreme, then this is an indication that you have low self-esteem.

case study SANJAY: JUMPING TO NEGATIVE CONCLUSIONS ABOUT YOURSELF

Sanjay is a student from a poor background who gets a relatively low test score in a practice test a few months before an important exam. His instinctive, automatic reaction to the test score is to think: 'I'm stupid' (negative thought about himself) and 'I'm going to fail the exam' (negative thought about the future).

Sanjay's negative thoughts lead him to feel highly anxious and downcast. The way in which he quickly draws a negative conclusion and general characterization of himself ('I'm stupid') from one poor test score illustrates his lack of self-esteem.

Part of Sanjay's negative characterization is that he sees himself as in some way inadequate and he thinks that getting a poor test score is unacceptable or shameful. He finds it difficult to accept himself if he doesn't achieve what he feels he should.

DEALING WITH NEGATIVE THOUGHTS ABOUT YOURSELF

Cognitive therapy, devised by Beck, encourages people to examine their negative thoughts and challenge or question possible distortions or exaggerations in their conclusions and viewpoint.

It is important to realize that cognitive therapy (and similarly cognitive behavioural therapy) does *not* say that if we have an automatic negative thought it is necessarily completely wrong or erroneous. What it does do is ask us to examine the evidence for our beliefs, to see if they are fully justified and if not then to moderate them in an appropriate manner.

case study SANJAY (CONTINUED): DEALING WITH NEGATIVE THOUGHTS

Using cognitive techniques with Sanjay, a therapist or coach might encourage him to look out for any exaggerations or distortions in his thoughts, to write down ways in which they were distorted and to then balance out the thoughts with more realistic statements to remind himself of the reality and put his situation in perspective. In such a context, Sanjay might come up with more realistic observations such as:

You could have done better in the test but it doesn't prove that you are stupid.

or:

You could fail the exam, but even if you do there will be an opportunity to retake it and if you seek advice from the tutor about where you went wrong you may be able to do better in the real exam.

Reminding himself of these more balanced statements could help Sanjay to take the edge off the feelings of despondency and negative thoughts he experiences and help him to approach the exam itself and the build-up to it in a more constructive way.

Here are some examples of balancing thoughts that people might create in particular situations to put self-critical thoughts in perspective:

> **Situation:** Sarah is watching TV with her partner John when he starts expressing his dislike of a politician who is speaking on the news. Sarah agrees with some of the politician's views and thinks John has described them inaccurately so she challenges his comments. John then walks out of the room.
> **Beliefs/thoughts:** 'I shouldn't have upset John by contradicting him.'
> **Feelings:** Guilty
> **Balancing thought created:** *It was reasonable for you to contradict John because you didn't agree with what he was saying.*

> **Situation:** Paul is working hard on a difficult piece of work his boss has given him.
> **Beliefs/thoughts:** 'I won't be able to finish this piece of work on time and my boss will be annoyed with me. I'm never able to get things done properly.'

Feelings: Annoyed with himself and stressed
Balancing thought created: *Do your best to finish the work on time but it's not the end of the world if you don't manage it.*

Situation: Linda comes home and finds her mum has visited unasked while she was out and moved some of her belongings around in the house while tidying up. She reacts angrily and shouts at her mum.
Beliefs/thoughts: 'I got angry with mum; that proves I am totally thoughtless.'
Feelings: Angry with herself and despondent
Balancing thought created: *Okay, you did something that you would prefer not to have done. You can't put the clock back but you can apologize to her and try to act differently if the situation arises again.*

Situation: Jean-Paul gives a presentation at a conference as part of his work. He forgets to make some of the points he had intended to. However, no one seems to notice and there are a series of questions at the end from interested participants, which he answers well.
Beliefs/thoughts: 'My presentation was useless. Everyone is going to think that I can't do the job.'
Feelings: Frustrated with himself

Balancing thought created: *Some people gave you good feedback. Others may have thought you could have done better but it's unlikely you'll please everyone. This is an aspect of your job that you know you find difficult, but everyone has different strengths and there is no real evidence to suggest that people think you can't do the job.*

Situation: Serena is frustrated by something one of her friends has done and mentions it in conversation with another friend, Tamsin, but she only receives a cursory response.

Beliefs/thoughts: 'Tamsin didn't look at me when I was speaking and just responded with a quiet "yes". Therefore she obviously didn't agree with what I said. I always say too much. I have offended her.'

Feelings: Anxious, guilty

Balancing thought created: *It's possible that Tamsin didn't like what you said but there are other possible explanations of her response. For example, she might have been thinking of something else completely and you could be jumping to conclusions.*

You can create balancing thoughts for past situations or events to help you come to terms with them and feel better about them. You can also use balancing thoughts in the present when difficult situations and negative or self-critical thoughts arise.

HOW TO CREATE BALANCING THOUGHTS

The first way to create balancing thoughts is simply to remind yourself that what you are trying to do is to create a realistic statement that you can say to yourself to help you put into perspective any negative or self-critical thoughts that you have and then come up with some suggestions and see if they do indeed put the original negative thought in a more realistic perspective.

If, however, you find it difficult to generate balancing thoughts by that initial method, then a second method you can use is to go through the five key questions in the *disputation checklist* (pages 67–9), and see if doing that helps you to come up with any helpful balancing thoughts that you can say to yourself in the relevant situation.

Another way of creating balancing thoughts is to use the ACCEPT acronym below which I have created to help clients memorize different ways of generating a more accepting attitude towards yourself. Some of the ways outlined in the ACCEPT acronym overlap with questions in the *disputation checklist* but the acronym may help you to remember them more easily.

USING THE ACCEPT ACRONYM TO HELP YOU CREATE AN ATTITUDE OF SELF-ACCEPTANCE

If you find yourself adopting a non-accepting attitude towards things you do or don't do, or thinking self-critical thoughts, write down exactly what your thought is then use one or more of the techniques indicated below to create and write down a balancing thought to say to yourself to help you put the original negative thought in perspective:

Accept yourself:

> i.e. Don't be so hard on yourself. What would you say to yourself if you were being a little more forgiving towards yourself? Write this down as your balancing thought and say it to yourself.

Counsel a friend:

> What would you say to a friend in your situation or what would a good friend say to you? Write this down as your balancing thought.

Constructive approach:

> If you were asked to say what positives might come out of the situation or what you might learn from it, what would you say? Write these comments down as your balancing thought.

Explore alternatives:

What alternative interpretations might there be of the actions, behaviour or events that are leading you to jump to negative conclusions about yourself? Could your negative judgement about yourself be a bit exaggerated? What would be a more balanced or moderate interpretation of the significance of the situation? Write this down as your balancing thought.

Prepare for the worst:

Face your fears! Imagine that the worst were to happen – how serious would it *really* be on a scale of 1–10 compared to other possible life events? And how could you respond to it if it did happen? Write down your assessment of seriousness and of how you could react or deal with the eventuality as your balancing thought.

Try to focus on something else:

Is it really worth expending all your emotional and mental energy over this issue? If you can't resolve the situation in your mind then consider doing something active or focusing on something else altogether for a short time, to give your mind some respite from circular or unproductive thoughts that may be affecting your self-belief and feelings of self-worth. This isn't really a balancing thought as such – it is an action. You can say things to yourself such as '*STOP!*' or snap an elastic band on your wrist to help you snap out of the cycle of negative thoughts and then make an effort to find something to occupy yourself and your mind, such as exercise or a crossword or work.

THE IMPORTANCE OF PRACTICE

Coaches or therapists who use CBT techniques and principles often stress the importance of practice (Beck in particular emphasizes the importance of adopting an experimental attitude and trying out some of the ideas or techniques to see how you get on with them). Practise creating balancing thoughts over a period of time until it has become second nature. The aim is not to get rid of negative or self-critical thoughts but to find a method for helping to manage them and put them in perspective, which in turn will help you to feel better about yourself and act in more constructive ways.

As a first step, try observing what you are thinking and recording any self-critical thoughts on a daily basis for a week or two using Ellis's ABC model (pages 64–6) then creating balancing thoughts for each self-critical thought using the methods described above. Read the balancing thoughts through to yourself to remind yourself to keep your self-criticism in perspective. If there are particular patterns that emerge, then try to remind yourself when one of those patterns is emerging and instead of getting harsh with yourself for allowing it to happen again, be kinder on yourself. Acknowledge that the pattern is coming up again and remind yourself of the balancing thought that you have created to deal with it.

Be patient with yourself – negative and self-critical thought patterns tend to become habitual. So to 'unlearn' them, be prepared to practise this technique for a while.

Congratulate yourself each time you find a balancing thought that helps you!

If you forget to use a balancing thought or it doesn't work so well on another occasion, don't be overly critical of yourself. Have a break (literally, go and do something relaxing if possible) or else reflect on whether there is anything you can try out instead next time which might help you to remember to use the balancing thought or to devise a different one that might in fact work better for you in the situation.

ANALYZING NEGATIVE THOUGHTS

For some people the balancing thoughts technique may be effective enough to deal with the situations where you are experiencing negative thoughts. However, if you find that you want to understand in greater detail what patterns you are getting into with your negative thoughts, so as to change them in a more precise way, then CBT can offer a number of specific ways of classifying different types of **distorted thinking patterns** that you may find helpful.

Bear in mind that if you find some or all of the following 'distorted thinking' patterns apply to you, you don't need to perceive this as a particular problem that you alone have – most people experience these kinds of difficulty to a greater or lesser degree, and most people can benefit from understanding which specific types of distorted thinking most apply to them, so that they can then learn to correct them, redress the balance, feel and act better.

THINKING FLEXIBLY AND CREATIVELY

Below I list some different types of distorted thinking patterns that can occur and make some suggestions as to the types of approach that might help you if you feel that a particular thinking pattern is one which you have a tendency towards:

All or nothing thinking (all-good or all-bad thinking): This involves extremes of thinking, without recognizing that realities may have shades of complexity or colour to them, e.g. thinking that something is perfect or else it is hopeless, that someone is a demon or else they are a saint.

What to try:

- Think of some in-between possibilities, if you can.

- Acknowledge that most people (whether you or someone else) have some good characteristics and some not-so-good characteristics. Be prepared to identify both sides to people (please note the exception to this: if your personal safety or that of someone you know is threatened by someone else then I advise you to take sensible steps to protect yourself – in these extreme cases safety may come before balance).

- Acknowledge that you may not have all the information needed to understand a situation fully and be prepared to suspend judgement if this is the case.

Mind-reading: This involves *assuming* that other people are thinking certain things about you or doing things for a particular reason, without having sufficient evidence to justify the assumption.

What to try:

- If the person you are making the assumption about is in conversation with you or is acting in a certain way, try to generate some alternative possible explanations for what the other person is doing or saying and then evaluate which of the alternative explanations seems most reasonable. If there are some which are equally likely or you don't know all the facts then acknowledge this.

- If you are imagining that someone who is not actually talking to you but is present with you (for example in a work or social situation) is thinking badly of you, remember that other people may have their own problems and may not be thinking about you at all.

- Imagine purely for the sake of argument that you *are* right about the explanation of the other person's behaviour. Try to clarify for yourself why that matters so much to you – then ask yourself what is the most constructive response you can have even if your assumption is right.

Fortune-telling or catastrophizing: Imagining that the worst is going to happen or making negative predictions in your mind.

What to try:

- Ask yourself what the evidence is to support your view that the worst will happen and what evidence there is that more positive outcomes might happen.

- What do you think is the percentage likelihood that the feared event may happen?

- What can you do to decrease the prospect of it happening?

- What can you do or say to yourself to help you cope if the feared event does happen?

Generalizing: This involves making sweeping statements that don't allow for exceptions, like: 'Why do I always …?' or 'Why do I never …?' This might be a thought about yourself or about someone else or about a certain group of people, e.g. men or women or people from a particular culture, religion or region.

What to try:

- Ask yourself if a more moderate claim might be more accurate, e.g. 'I *sometimes* …' or 'I *often* …'.

- Try to be fair, reasonable and accurate in your assessments of yourself as well as of others.

- Evaluate the evidence for and against the proposition you are making and ask yourself if it *really* justifies the sweeping generalization.

Labelling people and situations: This involves categorizing people according to extreme labels (usually negative labels, although excessively positive labels can also lead to problems when a person is not be able to live up to your fantasy of them). You might apply a label to yourself and/or to others – both can feed into low self-esteem. Examples might include accusing yourself or someone else of being: 'hopeless' or 'useless' or 'a failure' or 'self-centred'.

What to try:

- Remember that people and even situations are complex and that you too, just like anyone else, have some good and some not so good qualities.

- Allow for degrees and the possibility that some people (including yourself) may be good at some things and not so good at others.

- Allow others to be imperfect sometimes.

- If you are applying a negative label to someone else, then consider giving the person you are applying it to the possibility to comment on it. If you do make your point to them, then see if there is a way in which you can get it across which avoids over-generalization – e.g. comment on how they *behaved* in a particular situation and ask how they might behave differently if the situation occurs again.

- If you insist on applying a negative label to yourself or others and you are sure your perception is correct, then decide what your options are for dealing with the situation and how you want to respond. If you have a tendency to think of yourself as a victim, instead ask what your options are and pick the most constructive one if you can.

- If you are applying a negative label to yourself then ask what you can do to create at least *some* situations when the negative label doesn't apply to your behaviour. You don't have to fit that label *all* the time.

'Must', 'should' and 'ought' thoughts (making unreasonable demands of yourself or others): Again, the judgements may relate to others or to yourself.

What to try:

- Try to avoid dogmatic moralistic words like 'must', 'should' and maybe try out 'wish', 'prefer', 'want' or other words which reflect your feelings and wishes rather than impose a demand on yourself or on others.

- If you have a tendency to place too many demands on yourself then before committing yourself to doing something, weigh up the advantages and disadvantages of different responses and then choose the one that you think is most sensible rather than automatically trying to please everyone or do everything.

- Remind yourself that you have a right to some time for yourself and for meeting your own needs.

- If you are placing demands on someone else, then ask yourself, will it be *helpful* if I impose demands or expectations (whether in word or thought)? An alternative might be to make a request or slightly to lower your expectations of the other person (and of yourself as well if you expect to be always perfect in a particular role). None of us is perfect.

- Retain your own standards, ideals and preferences but try not to *insist* that the world (or you) always operate by them or *should* do so, as the world may not agree! Instead, acknowledge simply that you would *prefer* or *like* it if the world or another person (or yourself) acted differently (this is the tip given by Albert Ellis, mentioned earlier in this chapter under the sub-heading 'Changing prescriptions into preferences', page 61).

- If another person's behaviour is obviously aggressive or harmful, don't collude with that, but ask yourself what options you have to help you prevent the harmful effects or change the situation.

Emotional reasoning: You feel a certain way so you assume that your feeling must be justified by the situation, e.g. you feel like a failure so you assume you are one.

What to try:

- Examine the actual evidence for and against your interpretation of the situation and rate the likelihood of alternatives.

- Ask yourself what a friend whose judgement you trust would say about the situation.

- Remind yourself that just because you are unhappy with one of your actions or with a situation doesn't mean that you are totally flawed or that the situation will always apply.

- Think of some counter-examples where you might feel the same way but a different explanation is correct rather than the one you assume.

- If you have a tendency towards emotional reasoning, remind yourself of that and pause before making an evaluation.

Self-downing: You continually put yourself down.

What to try:

- Remind yourself of some of the affirmations you created in chapter 1.

- Ask yourself what a good friend would say to you in this situation.

- Make a mental note that you are about to put yourself down and decide not to.

- Aim for a small improvement next time rather than perfection.

Discounting the positives: You only see the negatives about yourself or your actions, not any positives.

What to try:

- Remind yourself of some of the affirmations you created in chapter 1.

- Ask yourself what a good friend would say to you in this situation.

- Ask yourself what you would say if you had to reframe the negative thought so as to find a positive in the situation.

try it now

Keep a record of times when you have a negative self-critical thought and specify in it:

1. What the negative thought is

2. What type of distorted thinking pattern or patterns are involved

3. A balancing thought to use to deal with the negative thought – use any of the techniques mentioned previously to create your balancing thought.

Once you have got an idea of particular negative thinking patterns that you have a tendency towards, then create a plan covering:

1. The type(s) of negative thinking you have a tendency towards

2. Examples of the kinds of situation where you tend to think that way

3. A plan for what you are going to try to do if you find yourself thinking that way.

Below is a sample plan that you might create:

Type of negative thinking pattern: Mind-reading

Example of a situation where I might think in this way: When I am in a meeting at work or in an unfamiliar social situation with people I don't know, I tend to think that people must be thinking that I don't know what I am doing or that I am awkward and look nervous.

Plan for what I might do if I find myself thinking in this way:

- Remind myself that other people have their own problems and may not be thinking of me or noticing me at all.
- Ask myself what other less negative possibilities there might be for what the other people are thinking and evaluate which is most likely. Or, if I just can't tell, acknowledge that.

Type of negative thinking pattern: Fortune-telling/catastrophizing

Example of a situation where I might think in this way: If I am in a relationship I tend to predict that it is going to go wrong and imagine the worst for fear of the other person rejecting me.

Plan for what I might do if I find myself thinking in this way:

- Ask myself what evidence there is to support the view that the worst will happen and what evidence there is that more positive outcomes might happen.
- Remind myself of positives in the relationship.
- Recognize that even if the worst does happen then I will be able to cope.
- Do other things to build up a balanced life, which helps me not to be dependent on approval or validation from that one person.

Type of negative thinking pattern: Making unreasonable demands on myself

Example of a situation where I might think in this way: If someone asks me to do something for them, I tend to think that I should do what they are asking to please them.

Plan for what I might do if I find myself thinking in this way:

- Pause before agreeing to do things I am not sure I want to do.
- Weigh up the advantages and disadvantages of different responses and choose a response on the basis of that analysis rather than automatically trying to please everyone or do everything.
- Remind myself that I have a right to some time for myself and for meeting my reasonable needs.

If there are other types of 'negative thinking' that you think apply to you, or you have your own strategies that you know or believe may work for you, then feel free to put those in too. You don't have to follow just the possible strategies I have given – the ideas I have given are suggestions that can be helpful but they are not the only ones.

USEFUL TIP

Remember you are trying to achieve practical results for you, not to get locked into a mindset about what is right and wrong – if you can, focus on what is *helpful* for you in the situation, not on whether you or someone else is right or wrong.

If you find that something you try out is useful then try it again. If not, then try something different. Remember that you can't usually learn without making some mistakes, so don't think you have to get it right first time and always. There is a famous saying used in the related field of neuro-linguistic programming (NLP): '*There is no such thing as failure, only feedback.*'

KEEPING A DIARY

Some people may feel that the idea of classifying your negative thoughts into different types is a little *too* analytical or scientific. If you find that that applies to you, then an alternative method of recording your thoughts is to keep a diary. This can be set out in a number of different ways. Whatever format you use for the diary, it is important that you make a note as accurately as possible of any significant negative thoughts that go through your head and the feelings that go with them so that you can then use the *disputation checklist* (page 67) or the ACCEPT acronym (pages 78–80) to help you create balancing thoughts for the negative thoughts.

USEFUL TIP
You can also if you want make a note of any *positive* thoughts in your diary. This can help to clarify positive points in the day that you may overlook (most of us have a tendency to focus on and remember the negative, so it helps to remind ourselves of the positive too). Provided that the positive thoughts are reasonably balanced and sensible and not excessive or distorted, they can help to counter-balance the negative thoughts.

(If your 'positive' thoughts are *extreme* and *unrealistic*, which may apply for example to people who experience bipolar disorder, then part of your approach may instead involve moderating or balancing *overly* positive thoughts, to put them in reasonable perspective. Since this book is primarily aimed at people who have low self-esteem and associated negative thoughts or self-critical attitudes, I don't discuss inappropriately positive thoughts in this book. However, it is worth bearing in mind that CBT is about balancing unrealistic or distorted thinking and that this can apply to overly positive thoughts just as to overly negative thoughts – some of the types of distorted thinking such as generalizing can apply as much to excessively positive thinking as to excessively negative thinking. Other types such as self-downing don't apply to overly positive thoughts – you are more likely to be prone to over-grandiose thoughts about yourself if you think *too* positively.)

In your diary, also give an overall rating for how you felt on each day that the diary covers. Then at a later stage, say in a few weeks, you will be able to check your records to see any changes in your general level of positive/negative feelings. Also, by giving a daily rating you will be able to see across the course of a week the extent to which your feelings are up and down. (**Note:** rating your feelings is very different from rating yourself *globally*, which Ellis spoke against – see pages 55–7. It is a legitimate, helpful piece of self-observation which can be useful.)

Things your diary could cover each day include:

1. What you did during the day

2. Your mood or feelings at different times in the day

3. The situations or circumstances when you felt that way

4. Any thoughts that went through your mind when you were in that mood/experiencing that feeling

5. An overall rating of how you felt during the day (out of 10).

case study CLAIRE: USING A DIARY TO ADDRESS NEGATIVE FEELINGS AND THOUGHTS

Claire has a tendency towards negative feelings about herself and her abilities. A few weeks ago she separated from her partner Pete. She has been preoccupied by that and also has had worries about her job. She has decided to create a diary to help her keep issues in perspective and cope with negative thoughts about herself. In the diary she includes the five elements listed above. Here are the entries from her first day of keeping the diary:

Day 1

Didn't sleep very well – got up late and arrived ten minutes late for work. Felt annoyed with myself and worried I might get into trouble. Thinking thoughts like: *Why am I always late? I'm so disorganized. They must all think I'm useless at work. What if my supervisor reports me?*

Set myself five tasks to get through in the day – found it difficult to concentrate – kept thinking about Pete leaving me. Only managed to get through three of the tasks.

Feeling angry and ashamed about how the relationship ended. Thinking: *Why do I always muck up in relationships? Am I always going to be alone? How stupid I must have been not to realize Pete was seeing someone else.*

I reminded myself of what Jo said about how many relationships fail and about some of my positive qualities. It did help a bit – not good that so many relationships fail, but at least I'm not the only one!

Went for a walk in the lunch break, trying to clear my head. Felt a bit more relaxed and was able to work a bit better in the afternoon. My supervisor didn't come over and seemed to be looking at his work all the time. I wondered: *Is he deliberately avoiding me? I know the firm is struggling at the moment. Perhaps I'm going to lose my job.*

Spent the evening watching TV – still thinking about the end of my relationship and feeling frustrated: *I ought to be able to shake this off – it's been three weeks now. I want to move on.* Eventually found a rerun of some old comedy – actually got me laughing a bit, although strangely I almost felt annoyed with myself in finding I could forget about the relationship even if for only twenty minutes!

Went to bed at 10.30pm – trying to get in a healthy routine.

Overall rating for how I felt during the day (out of 10): 3

MAKING USE OF YOUR DIARY

Once you have started recording your feelings, thoughts and actions in a diary, you can start to make use of it by going through and creating balancing thoughts (using any of the techniques described earlier in the chapter) for any negative thoughts you have noted down, to put them in perspective or help you realize when the negative thought is distorted or exaggerated.

case study CLAIRE (CONTINUED): CREATING BALANCING THOUGHTS TO USE IN RELATION TO HER DIARY

Claire's balancing thoughts after going through her diary are set out below. At the end of the exercise she has also added a 'constructive comment' on the day, which you can also do.

Negative thought: 'Why am I always late? I'm so disorganized. They must all think I'm useless at work.'

Balancing thought: *Actually you've had good performance reviews. It's true that time-keeping is not your strong point. You can concentrate on improving it starting with the next week but it doesn't mean that you are useless – the feedback you get shows you are highly regarded.*

Negative thought: 'Why do I always muck up in relationships? … How stupid I must have been not to realize Pete was seeing someone else.'

Balancing thought: *Relationships are hard – many fail and others continue but in a very bad state. Yes, some are good and* *that's what you want but there's no point in being too hard on yourself. Maybe you could have realized what was happening earlier but being overly suspicious wouldn't necessarily have helped.*

Negative thought: 'Is my supervisor avoiding me? ... Perhaps I'm going to lose my job.'

Balancing thought: *There are other possible explanations of why your supervisor seemed preoccupied – perhaps he has his own problems or perhaps he is just focusing on his own work! Anyway, if the worst happens and you lose your job, it's not actually the end of the world.*

Negative thought: 'Why do I keep thinking about the end of the relationship? I ought to be able to shake off these thoughts. It's been three weeks now. I want to move on.'

Balancing thought: *What happened was stressful and it's normal that you will think about it for some time. Three weeks is not long. You can try to find other things to focus on but it will take time. Be patient!*

Constructive comment at the end of the day: *Although I was tired and stressed, and indulged in some negative thoughts which didn't help, I still did some sensible things – like taking a break at lunch to clear my head. I got through the day despite my worries and I even managed to laugh at a TV programme and forget about my problems for twenty minutes.*

LOOKING FOR PATTERNS IN YOUR DIARY

Another thing you can try if you are using a diary like Claire is to look over your diary entries over a period of days, looking out for anything you are doing which is helping you to feel better and act more positively. Unless there are significant downsides to those actions which outweigh the positives, make a commitment to trying them again in similar situations.

try it now

If you start to use a diary in a similar way to Claire, or if you are keeping any other kind of record of your thoughts, feelings and actions over a period of time, look through your entries for a few days then write down your answers to the five questions listed below. If this gives you some ideas for what might help to raise your self-esteem in a helpful way then try to apply those ideas:

1. What activities do you find make your mood worse or do not help your situation?

2. What activities do you find can help your mood in a reasonable way without significant adverse consequences? (**Note:** Do *not* include in your answer activities which have a significant negative aspect or subsequent negative consequence such as drinking excessive amounts of alcohol, which can lift your mood initially but then acts as a depressant drug and is likely to worsen your feelings overall.)

3. What ways of reacting to situations do you find make the situations worse?

4. What ways of reacting to situations do you find tend to help?

5. What new activities or new ways of reacting might you try out to help with your situation?

SUCCESS, ASPIRATIONS AND SELF-ESTEEM

One thing that Claire's diary graphically indicates is that you can put a lot of pressure on yourself if you feel that you must be successful in work, relationships or other particular spheres of life. If you place too much importance on success, then if you think you have failed this can be damaging for your self-esteem.

William James, an American psychologist who lived in the second half of the 19th century, is often cited as a forerunner of interest in self-esteem in modern times. James presented self-esteem in a formula:

$$\text{Self-esteem} = \frac{\text{Success}}{\text{Pretensions}}$$

(from *The Principles of Psychology* by William James, Chapter X: The Consciousness of Self, 1890).

By 'pretensions' James means your aspirations or goals. In other words his view was that your self-esteem will increase if you are successful in achieving your goals and will be even higher if you achieve more than you aspire to. On this view, however, if you *don't* succeed in reaching your goals your self-esteem will suffer. In part, this chapter has been about showing what you can do to accept yourself if that situation arises and you do not meet your goals. Following James' formula through logically you can also see that if you want to increase your self-esteem it is sensible to set realistic goals rather than over-optimistic ones (which you might not have much chance of achieving). However, I would suggest that you don't want to set your goals *too* low or you may lose all motivation! It's about achieving a sensible balance.

The ideas of Albert Ellis and Aaron Beck, as indicated in this chapter, suggest that achieving a balanced view about your own failures or imperfections, instead of attaching too much importance to success, may ultimately benefit you. This kind of balanced approach to yourself and your life can be a more secure route to a reasonable level of self-esteem than focusing all your attentions on achieving success. In the next chapter we will be looking at another aspect of achieving balance in your life – *looking after yourself*.

REMEMBER: KEY IDEAS FROM CHAPTER 2

Some of the key ideas from chapter 2 are:

- Developing an attitude of self-acceptance involves recognizing that you can make mistakes without that meaning you are worthless.

- Developing an attitude of self-acceptance involves adopting a less judgemental attitude towards yourself.

- Practising detached observation of yourself, your thoughts and your feelings can be helpful for dealing with shame about yourself or your body.

- You can use the ABC model to help you analyze negative and self-critical thoughts.

- You can use a *disputation checklist* or the ACCEPT acronym to help challenge self-critical thoughts and create balancing thoughts to put them in perspective.

- You can analyze distorted thinking patterns into different types and use appropriate techniques to tackle the types of distorted thinking that you may have a tendency towards.

- Keeping a diary focusing on balancing out negative thoughts can be helpful for your self-acceptance and related self-esteem.

CHAPTER 3

Look after yourself

*'The needs of a human being are sacred. Their
satisfaction cannot be subordinated either to
reasons of state, or to any consideration of money,
nationality, race or colour, or to the moral or
other value attributed to the human being in
question, or to any consideration whatsoever.'*

—Simone Weil,
Draft for a Statement of Human Obligations (1943)
(translation by Richard Rees)

So far I have considered the first two elements of the
VALUE acronym for improving your self-esteem, *value
yourself* and *accept yourself*. The third element is about
looking after yourself.

WHY LOOKING AFTER YOURSELF IS IMPORTANT IF YOU HAVE LOW SELF-ESTEEM

If you don't value yourself very highly then you may be
inclined to ignore your own needs or wishes or put them
behind those of others. In some cases you may even feel
that you don't deserve to do things that you want to do or

that are beneficial to you, or that you deserve to experience hardship. If this happens, then it can lead you either to think that you *have to* or *must* put everyone else's needs before your own or that there is no point in you making an effort to do very much because you are not worth it. In either case the potential result is that you end up not looking after yourself and your basic mental and physical health is disregarded, as illustrated in the following flow chart:

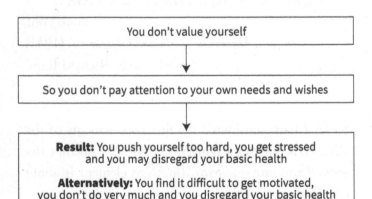

A TWOFOLD APPROACH TO LOOKING AFTER YOURSELF

There are two approaches which can help you to deal with this kind of issue, if you suffer from low self-esteem and are consequently not paying sufficient attention to your own needs and wishes:

1. Try to address the underlying *thought patterns* about yourself and what you deserve that are leading you not to value yourself by using the techniques described in the previous two chapters and in the following two chapters (on *understanding yourself* and *empowering yourself*).

2. If you have identified that this is an issue for you, then make an active attempt to look after yourself in your *actions*. This chapter is aimed at showing you what this might involve and encouraging you to try to make that conscious effort to look after yourself and achieve a healthy life balance if a lack of self-esteem has meant that up until now you have not been doing that.

MASLOW'S HIERARCHY OF NEEDS

Abraham Maslow, an American professor of psychology in the 20th century, proposed a theory of human needs and motivation that can provide a helpful starting point for thinking about what areas of your life you are ignoring or downplaying. In the most advanced version of his theory, Maslow set out a number of categories of basic needs ('deficiency needs') and also a number of categories of higher order needs ('growth needs') relating to personal growth and development.

The types of needs Maslow described are as follows:

DEFICIENCY NEEDS (BASIC NEEDS):

- *Physiological needs* – basic biological needs, such as the need for oxygen, water, food. Also the need for sleep, sexual needs and the need to avoid pain.

- *Safety and security needs* – the need for security, stability, protection from harm, perhaps also the need for a stable job or income and a home.

- *Love and belonging needs* – the need for relationships of different kinds: family, friends, romance, community.

- *Esteem needs* – the need to have the respect of others and the need for self-respect, self-confidence, independence and freedom.

GROWTH NEEDS (RELATING TO PERSONAL GROWTH AND DEVELOPMENT):

- *The need to know and understand* – the need to gain knowledge and understand the world and one's environment.

- *Aesthetic needs* – the need for symmetry, balance and beauty.

- *Self-actualization needs* – the need to achieve one's potential and find fulfilment.

- *Transcendence* – the need to connect to something beyond the ego or to help others find fulfilment and realize their potential.

You don't have to agree with Maslow's account of the hierarchical order of human needs, with some being seen as basic and others as relating to personal growth, to be able to make use of it, although it is interesting to note that Maslow classed esteem as being among the basic needs. In my view, the best way to think of Maslow's analysis is as a starting point for your own reflections about what could be helpful for you to focus on:

try it now

Look through the categories of needs described by Maslow and answer the following questions for yourself:

1. Which category of needs do you most want to meet better in your life now?

2. What will be the potential impact on other categories of needs from you doing so?

3. What sort of balance do you want to achieve between the different categories of needs? (To what degree do you want to shift your current priorities?)

4. What would be the potential consequences of shifting your priorities?

5. What specific actions can you commit to over the next week in the light of your answers to the four questions above?

KEEPING A HEALTHY, BALANCED LIFESTYLE

Maintaining a healthy, balanced lifestyle is a sensible thing to do whether or not you experience low self-esteem, because of the benefits it brings to your mental and physical well-being. However, if you are experiencing low self-esteem and related anxiety about yourself or what you are doing, then there is often a strong emotional and psychological pull on you to focus all your time and energy on trying to do better or more. It is then all too easy to forget to keep up the basic principles of living a healthy lifestyle.

If anything, it is even more important in these circumstances to keep up with a healthy lifestyle, because the more your body and mind are out of balance, the harder you will find it to approach your anxiety in a balanced way and to respond to it sensibly and practically. Below are some **basic principles for keeping a healthy balanced lifestyle**:

1. Following healthy routines: Try to:

- Eat a balanced, healthy diet with regular meal times.

- If possible, follow a regular sleep pattern, getting up at a similar time each day and going to bed at a similar time each night.

- Do a reasonable amount of moderate exercise (you don't have to run a marathon – half an hour's walk five days per week would be sufficient).

- Avoid drinking alcohol to excess (and don't drink it in order to relieve anxiety – that may give you instant relief for a short period but once the initial effect wears off it will make the anxiety worse and your sleep may well suffer too).

2. Paying attention to priorities: If there is a possibility that you may be stressing your mind and body by trying to do too much, then it is important that you:

- Reflect on what is important to you and try to focus on those priorities.

- With regard to tasks that are less important which you do perhaps by habit, evaluate what the consequences would be if you did less of them – if the consequences would not in fact be too bad then make a decision as to whether you are going to cut down and if so by how much.

3. Giving yourself permission to relax: If you spend ten to twelve hours a day working, or alternatively if you are on the go all the time in some other way such as doing household tasks and supporting a family without any opportunity for a break, then the chances are that you are not carrying out your tasks as productively as you could. You may also be putting excessive strain on your mind and body. At some point this is likely to show in the form of ill health, moodiness, anxiety or in other ways, so if possible build short breaks into your day to keep yourself refreshed. Arrange some times in the week when you are going to do something you want to do.

DEALING WITH ANXIOUS OR GUILTY THOUGHTS

If you find that anxious or guilty thoughts are getting in the way of you living a balanced lifestyle then use some of the techniques described in other chapters to help manage those thoughts, such at the balancing thoughts techniques outlined in chapter 2.

General principles to remember if you find yourself thinking that you should be doing certain things that you are not doing, or if you think that you should be doing them better, or if you think that you can't possibly stop doing them (even though they are harming your health or life balance) are as follows:

- Try to be kinder to yourself and try to put criticism in perspective.

- Remember that nobody is perfect.

- Acknowledge your weaknesses and try to do something about them if you can in a practical way, but before you go on too extensive a self-improvement programme, ask yourself just how serious those weaknesses are – do they significantly harm or hamper you or others or are they just minor blemishes? If the latter, then remind yourself of that – give yourself a break! Of course, if you think that your weaknesses really may amount to serious problems, such as a mental disorder or a damaging level of alcohol use or a tendency to violence, then seek help from an appropriate professional.

- Identify your strengths and be proud of them (see the part of chapter 1 that deals with creating affirmations). See if you can put your strengths or interests to use in a creative way to help manage the issues that are worrying you.

REMEMBER

Research suggests that you have a greater chance of achieving changes in your routine if you set yourself **specific goals** and keep a record of your progress:

- Set yourself daily or weekly goals that are achievable and realistic.

- Write down your commitment to achieving them.

- Keep a record of how well you do in respect of the goals you set.

- Reward yourself if you achieve your goals.

- If you fall short on a goal, don't punish yourself. Re-evaluate whether the goal needs to be modified or changed and if there are ways you can increase your chances of achieving it (by for example, putting it in a calendar or by telling someone of it), then try to do that to help you achieve the new or modified goal.

case study ANDY: IMPROVING LIFE BALANCE

Andy has suffered from low self-esteem ever since he can remember. This is fuelled by high levels of anxiety. He runs his own building company and finds himself frequently worrying about whether customers are going to complain about work he had done (his standards and competence are actually very professional). He employs several labourers to work for him and finds that much of his day is spent in rushing backwards and forward to different jobs they are working on to check on their work or deal with minor problems as they arise. He works about 60 hours in a week and rarely has a break. After reflecting on his lack of life balance and the fact that although he has quite a high level of income he rarely gets the chance to use it, Andy sets himself the following short-term goals:

- To promote one of his more experienced labourers to the role of foreman, thus freeing up some of his own time

- To make sure that he has at least a half-hour lunch break each day

- To set aside two evenings each week for doing a leisure activity that he wants to do

- To make a list of the tasks that he might usually do himself in a week and to delegate any of those that he doesn't actually have to do himself.

Andy finds it quite difficult at first to carry out the above aims but after writing out his commitment and evaluating at the end of each day whether he has stuck to it, he finds that he is beginning to get used to the more balanced approach. He notices that he feels less stressed and that he has more energy to devote to important tasks as well as to the things he wants to do. Consequently he feels more positive about himself and his work.

try it now

Read through pages 110–12 on keeping a healthy, balanced life-style, then answer the following questions:

1. What aspects of a healthy, balanced lifestyle do you think you do to some degree already?

2. What aspects of a healthy, balanced lifestyle do you think you could most improve on?

3. In light of your answers to the above, list three aspects of life balance that you are going to commit to trying to implement in the next seven days (these might be positive things you already do that you are going to continue or they might be changes that you are going to try to make in your lifestyle). Set yourself a specific action to undertake in respect of each aspect.

KEEPING UP WITH DAY-TO-DAY ACTIVITIES

In the flow chart at the start of this chapter (page 106) I suggested that not valuing yourself may lead to you not taking care of yourself in one of two ways – either by leading you to push yourself too hard and not take care of life balance considerations such as those covered in the last few pages *or* by leading to you finding it difficult to get motivated. If the latter is the problem for you (i.e. if you are doing too little rather than too much) then it is easy to fall into the following cycle of feelings and actions:

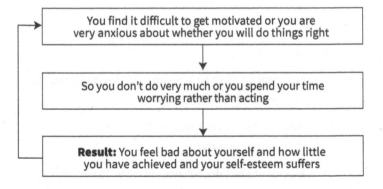

If this pattern applies to you, then often the best approach you can take, although it is difficult, is to try to get back into a reasonable routine of activities, making sure that the routine you decide upon is achievable.

This will partly involve doing things that you like doing (as highlighted in the previous pages in relation to life balance) but it may also involve doing some more mundane regular daily activities – at least until you find something better to do. There are a number of reasons why it is good to keep up with day-to-day activities to a reasonable level (without overdoing it) if you have a tendency not to do very much and to spend the time worrying or feeling down:

1. Doing day-to-day activities can help to take your mind off anxious thoughts and lessen anxiety.

2. If you have become caught in a pattern of negative thoughts about yourself and it is causing you not to do very much, then if you can get back to something like normal activity you may well feel better about yourself and not feel so inadequate.

3. If you don't get back to normal activity then some tasks may build up, creating more problems and anxiety.

try it now CREATING AN ACTIVITIES SCHEDULE

List under the heading 'possible activities' any activities that you:

- Need to do during the week

- Would like to do if you had time

- Would do if you could relax

- Might do to give you some physical exercise (even if it's just walking to the shops).

After looking at your answers to the above, set yourself some specific actions to do during the next seven days, putting them in a schedule like the one below, to indicate when you plan to do them:

	Morning	Afternoon	Evening
Monday			
Tuesday			
Wednesday			
Thursday			
Friday			
Saturday			
Sunday			

USEFUL TIP
Try putting just one or two actions per day into the table at first. If you think that more than that may be unrealistic in your current situation then just leave your intended commitment at that level for the first week or two, or put other actions in but indicate that they are *optional* so that you can make a choice whether to do them or not when the time comes.

SUCCESS, PLEASURE AND MOTIVATION

If you find it hard to motivate yourself to create an activities schedule, then write out a list of potential benefits for you from carrying it out and remind yourself of those when you hesitate before doing a scheduled activity. Also keep your schedule to hand so that you can refer to it.

If your reason for hesitating before creating an activities schedule or doing some of the things on it is that you doubt that you can or will achieve them, then you may find it helpful to write out the reasons and ask yourself in each instance, 'What have I got to lose by trying it out?' or if it seems too much, 'Is there a way that I can reduce the action to a more achievable level?'

Aaron Beck, one of the developers of CBT (see page 70) also suggested that for people who are feeling depressed or doubtful of their ability to carry out tasks, it can be helpful to keep a record of each time you master an activity by noting 'M' for 'mastery' against it, or for each time you enjoy an activity by noting 'P' against it for 'pleasure'. (If you think that the word 'mastery' has an unnecessarily masculine connotation then using the letter 'S' to denote 'success' is an alternative notation system you can use.) Noting down your successes and pleasurable experiences can help to counter the natural tendency of people with low self-esteem or who are feeling down not to notice things that go well or that they enjoy but to dwell more on negatives.

case study RUBY: SCHEDULING ACTIVITIES

Ruby was recently made redundant from her job. For the first couple of weeks she found it quite a relief as she had been struggling to keep herself motivated in the job anyway, but as time passes and she is still unable to get work, she begins to worry more and do less and her self-esteem suffers.

Using an activities schedule, she creates a list of daily activities with a balance between those relating to job hunting, those relating to necessary but not particularly pleasurable tasks such as domestic chores, and those relating to enjoyable activities that she wants to do for herself but hasn't got round to. She creates the week's schedule on a Monday morning and at the end of each day she marks 'S' against those tasks she has successfully achieved and 'P' against those she has enjoyed. After the first week, she notes that her productivity has increased and also that the balance in the schedule enables her to do some things she likes without feeling guilty. She begins to feel more positive about herself and her prospects.

REMEMBER

If you are setting yourself a schedule of activities try to follow these principles:

- Be realistic – don't set yourself activities to fill every minute of the whole week if you know that realistically in your state of mind you would not be able to achieve half of them! Instead perhaps set one activity for the day, or one for the morning and one for the afternoon or whatever *you* think you can reasonably achieve in your current situation and state of mind.

- Aim to achieve a balance between things that you need to do and things that you enjoy doing.

- Remember when you schedule a programme of activities, it is okay to adjust the programme if circumstances change or if you realize your schedule is not realistic for you. Aim to have an experimental approach if you're not sure what to do: try out possible options, see how they work for you and adjust them if appropriate.

INSOMNIA AND SELF-ESTEEM

Daily activities and occupying yourself sensibly can help to raise your self-esteem and take your mind away from negative or self-critical thoughts. Another area where anxieties or negative thoughts about yourself could be affecting you adversely is in terms of sleep. If you are continually worrying about whether you have done the right thing or criticizing yourself for actions you have or have not taken, this can affect your ability to sleep. This can then become a vicious circle where your lack of sleep makes it harder for you to think clearly, contributes to your own negative thoughts and feelings and makes it difficult for you to act constructively and positively. It can be helpful to follow some basic principles to help you sleep better.

SLEEPING WELL – SOME SIMPLE TIPS

The occasional missed night's sleep may make you feel tired the next day, but it won't harm your health. However, if you frequently miss sleep this can lead to:

- Prolonged bouts of tiredness

- Difficulties concentrating and lack of productivity in daily tasks

- Irritability or anxiety, which may also affect the way you relate to others

- Feelings of depression and/or frustration and low self-esteem

- Poor judgement.

On average, adults need around eight hours' sleep per night but the amount of sleep needed can vary quite significantly for different individuals and you probably know best how much sleep is helpful for you and how you react if you have not had enough sleep.

If you frequently have difficulty sleeping, this may be due to:

- Practical causes, e.g. the bedroom being noisy or the bed being uncomfortable

- Psychological or emotional causes, e.g. worrying about something or feeling low

- Physical or physiological causes, e.g. illness, physical pain or the response of your body to your diet or to medication.

DO'S AND DON'TS FOR PEOPLE WHO HAVE DIFFICULTY SLEEPING

Do's:

- Go to bed at regular times and get up at regular times.

- Exercise moderately four to five hours before bedtime if possible (but not just before sleeping as that is likely to keep you awake).

- Establish a regular, relaxing routine just before you go to bed – for example, by using a simple relaxation exercise (some are given below – see pages 126–9).

- Sleep on a bed that is comfortable.

- Ensure as far as possible that your bedroom is not too hot or too cold or too noisy – for some people it can help to have relaxing music playing in the background when they fall asleep.

Don'ts:

- Don't drink anything with caffeine in it after early afternoon. Caffeine is a stimulant drug which can keep you awake and can stay in your body for up to eight hours (sometimes even longer) after your last drink of tea or coffee. It can also increase feelings of anxiety.

- Don't eat a lot shortly before you go to bed.

- Don't drink a lot of alcohol – it may help you to fall asleep initially, but it is likely to disturb the quality of your sleep and you may well wake up after getting to sleep initially.

- Try not to make up for lost sleep by sleeping during the next day or on the weekend if you have had a poor sleeping pattern or episode. This can make it harder to get to sleep the next night.

DEALING WITH WORRIES THAT KEEP YOU AWAKE

If you find that you are lying in bed worrying about something that may happen and that is preventing you getting to sleep, then you may find it helpful to get out of bed, go to another room and try the following:

1. Ask yourself what is the realistic likelihood of the event or situation that you are worrying about actually happening. If you give it a very high percentage, then ask yourself what percentage other people whose judgement you trust might give to the event happening. You can write down these estimates and who might make them. You don't need to decide which is correct.

2. Then ask yourself what is the worst that could happen *and* write down the most positive response that you could have to that if it did happen.

3. Next write down one or two simple things that you can do to reduce the likelihood of the event or situation you are worrying about happening, or to reduce its impact if it does happen, even if only in a small way. If you judge that there is nothing that you can do to reduce the likelihood of the event occurring, then acknowledge that the event may be beyond your control.

4. Finally, write down in a short statement of one to four sentences a summary of what you have learned from steps 1–3.

Once you have completed the exercise, try not to dwell on it but spend ten to twenty minutes (still in another room) on a distracting and relaxing activity such as watching television, listening to the radio or reading. Then return to bed. If helpful, practise a short relaxation technique before you get back into bed to help you unwind and relax – see below.

RELAXATION TECHNIQUES

If you are prone to negative or anxious thoughts about yourself then you may find it difficult to 'switch off'. That can make your stress worse and also impact on your ability to get to sleep. It can therefore be useful to learn some simple relaxation techniques, which you can use either regularly if you find it helpful to do so or else on specific occasions when you are feeling particularly stressed. The aim of the exercises is to help you switch off and to take your mind away from the immediate thoughts which might otherwise preoccupy you – so don't use the exercises in any environment where for health or safety reasons you need to concentrate fully on another task, such as when you are driving or operating machinery!

try it now

When you get a convenient opportunity, try out one of the relaxation exercises below.

Exercise A: counting backwards

Shut your eyes and start counting backwards from a number of your choosing. This might be 30 or 40 or whatever number you feel is realistic for you in the time frame you have allocated for the exercise. I would suggest that if you think you might want to use relaxation exercises as a part of your daily or weekly routine, then don't set yourself too high a number to count from if you feel that you will not be able to keep this up on a regular basis. It is better to build up gradually from a relatively low starting point than to set yourself a target that you are unlikely to be able to keep up. If you do find yourself losing impetus, then lower the target number.

Count backwards in the following way:

1. Breathe in slowly and deeply, filling your lungs (if you are breathing in a relaxed way from your diaphragm, ideally your stomach should be filling out as you breathe rather than your upper chest).

2. After your in-breath has finished, breathe out in the same slow, relaxed, measured manner.

3. At the end of your out-breath say to yourself the number you have reached.

4. Once your breath has expired you will naturally begin to breathe in again, without having to force yourself. Allow this natural process to take place and repeat the in-breath, followed by the out-breath, followed by the next number down.

5. Repeat this process until you have reached zero. You can if you wish, then repeat the whole process again, starting from your target number.

Note: If you find at any time that you lose count of where you are or that your concentration wanders, just draw yourself back into the exercise and resume counting at the last point you can remember.

Exercise B: tensing your toes

For this exercise you lie on your back and close your eyes, then:

1. Focus your attention on your toes and how they feel.
2. Flex your toes upwards towards your face and count slowly up to five.
3. Relax your toes.
4. Count slowly up to five again.

Repeat steps 1–4, eight to ten times.

Exercise C: guided imagery

For this exercise, decide how long you are going to do it for – perhaps five or ten minutes initially, or a bit longer if you wish and have time. Once you are in the comfortable setting and position that you have chosen for the exercise:

1. Shut your eyes and imagine yourself in a place or environment that you find enjoyable, doing something relaxing and pleasurable. This will vary depending on what you as an individual enjoy. You could, for example, be by a lake or the sea or in beautiful scenery, or you could imagine yourself socializing with good friends or on a journey. Whatever situation you choose, make sure it is a harmonious one and not connected with current activities or stresses. The exercise should take you into a relaxing world.

2. Once you are in that relaxing world, try to imagine it in as much detail as you can – what sounds can you hear, what sensations are you experiencing in your body, who or what else is there, what is happening between yourself and others or the environment?

After the time period you allowed for the session, open your eyes and resume your normal activities.

If there is a particular calm preparatory routine (e.g. putting on particular clothing, having a drink of water or adjusting the lighting level in the room) which you can establish and repeat so that you associate it with doing whichever relaxation exercise(s) you choose, then this can also help to engender the relaxation. On the other hand, avoid ingesting substances which might alter your mood or create health risks as part of the routine, except under medical advice, as these may have detrimental effects (for example, caffeine, alcohol, tobacco or other drugs).

REMEMBER: KEY IDEAS FROM CHAPTER 3
From the information in this chapter on *looking after yourself* I would particularly stress the following:

- If you have low self-esteem you may pay insufficient attention to your own physical and mental health, so it is important *consciously* to look after yourself.

- Make sure that you do some relaxing (but healthy) activities for yourself each week.

- Set yourself achievable goals and give yourself credit if you are successful in achieving them.

- Do some regular moderate exercise.

- If you are not feeling great about yourself, be wary of drinking alcohol to help you feel better or to try to relieve your stress or anxiety.

- Try using some simple relaxation exercises if you have difficulty sleeping and cut down on caffeine use.

CHAPTER 4

Understand yourself

*'I could be bounded in a nutshell and
count myself a king of infinite space were
it not that I have bad dreams.'*

—William Shakespeare, *Hamlet*,
Act II, Scene ii

IDENTIFYING PERSONAL CAUSES OF LOW SELF-ESTEEM

I recently received an email from someone interested in learning techniques for dealing with low self-esteem. The email is reproduced below (suitably adapted to avoid any prospect of identification). It highlights some notable background experiences of a person suffering from low self-esteem:

'I have a good job and am in a good situation, but I often think about things from my past and events where people were putting me down. I am the youngest of three children and when I was younger I always felt that people didn't take me seriously. I guess my parents didn't help because they were always nagging me, as parents often do, about one thing or another. My school was very academic and I am not very organized so people assumed I was not very clever. However, I did obtain a degree and professional qualifications and now I am quite successful, working in my dream job in a place I want to be, but I still have problems with self-esteem and confidence, which are affecting my day-to-day happiness. I was also bullied by my father when I was younger. We get on better now but I still feel angry about it. I think my brother and sister may feel the same way but we are not good about talking about feelings so I am not sure.'

The first point I would like to make about this email is that it shows (just in case anyone doubted it) that you can be in many respects capable and successful and still experience low self-esteem.

It is also clear from the email that the person who wrote it had a good degree of understanding of the possible causes of their low self-esteem and had already identified a number of them:

- Repeated experience of being put down

- Possible experience from being treated in a particular way within a family framework (in this case as a younger child)

- Criticism or 'nagging' from parents

- Negative messages from a school environment

- Bullying from a parental figure.

You will also probably have observed that notwithstanding their understanding of *why* they had developed low self-esteem, the person writing the email was still experiencing problems with it when they wrote. This is not surprising and certainly not something that the individual should be blamed for – if you have experiences that have a strong or persistent effect on you, they can live with you for a long time. What this does suggest however is that understanding *why* you have low self-esteem in itself may not be sufficient to help you deal with your low self-esteem effectively. A twofold approach is required:

1. Understanding why you have low self-esteem. This is often not rocket science but involves aspects of or events in your background or upbringing which you are aware of.

and

2. Learning ways of dealing with your low self-esteem or improving it.

Therefore this chapter covers not just understanding the reasons for your low self-esteem, but also some constructive ways of responding to that understanding.

POSSIBLE CAUSES OF LOW SELF-ESTEEM

As indicated in chapter 1 of this book, self-esteem is a part of your self-image and the way you look at and think about yourself.

Your self-image develops during childhood and is the combination of your own natural personality features together with the messages and influences you receive from those around you about how you should act and feel about yourself. Research suggests that the parenting style of your parents can play a significant role in your self-esteem as well as genetic factors. Other experiences such as being sexually or physically abused can, not surprisingly, also impact negatively on your self-esteem.

Below are some of the kinds of parenting or childhood experiences that may affect a person's self-esteem adversely:

- Parents who have unrealistic, high expectations of what their children should and can achieve (this and the other comments below relating to parenting apply equally to a child's primary care giver, even if they are not the child's biological parent)

- Parents who, whether for good or not-so-good reasons, apply excessive criticism, negative comparisons or labels to their children

- Parents who find it difficult to give appropriate warmth, love and acceptance to their children

- Parents who are too preoccupied with their own issues and concerns to be able to pay sufficient attention to the needs of their children

- Parents who themselves have low self-esteem and whose behaviour the child copies (usually unconsciously)

- Experience of abuse (emotional, psychological, sexual, physical, or through neglect)

- Rejection or factors similar to the above experienced at the hands of other children or from adults who play a part in the person's development (e.g. teachers or relatives).

It is important to realize however that not all individuals are affected in the same way. Just because any of the features described above were present in your childhood it doesn't follow that you will automatically develop low self-esteem and of course there may be other individual factors relevant to you personally that you can identify as causes or contributory factors for your own low or high self-esteem.

It is also possible to develop low self-esteem as an adult. If, for example, you experience a traumatic event or if you perform an action about which you subsequently feel guilty or ashamed.

SOCIETAL EXPECTATIONS AND DISCRIMINATION

Media messages and societal expectations or prejudices about your gender, race, sexual orientation, culture, physical disability, mental health or other features
can also play a part in giving or reinforcing a negative
self-image. However, some of the research that has been
done has suggested that the correlations are not as high
as you might expect and don't always work in an obvious way. For example, some research suggests that black
Americans, despite being discriminated against, may
have higher self-esteem than their white counterparts on
average, although some other racial minority groups such
as people with origins in Hispanic countries on average
appear to have lower self-esteem in research.

GENDER DIFFERENCES AND SELF-ESTEEM

Research suggests that on average females have slightly
lower self-esteem than males, particularly in the late
teens, but that the difference is not large. There is some
evidence to suggest that when women report their
experiences in relation to self-esteem they tend to focus
more on whether or not other people accept or reject
them than men do and that men tend to focus more
than women on experiences of success and failure (this is
discussed further below). It is worth remembering however that these statistical differences will not apply to

everyone: there are plenty of women and men who would not fit in a simple way into the gender label implied by this distinction.

ASPIRATIONS RELATIVE TO A PARTICULAR GROUP

As indicated above, the common thought that discrimination is likely to cause lower self-esteem is not evidenced in a straightforward way by research. In his book *Self-Esteem: Research, Theory and Practice*, Chris Mruk suggests that one of a number of possible explanations of this, at least in relation to racial, ethnic or economic groups, is that if you meet the aspirations that are deemed worthy by those within the culture or subculture that you identify with, then your self-esteem can be high irrespective of whether or not you are discriminated against by society at large. On this basis, for example, a well-respected figure within a particular ethnic minority community might have reasonable self-esteem because of their standing within their community even if they face discrimination from people outside that community. Similarly, a person who is born deaf may face discrimination from outside the deaf community but be well respected within the deaf community and have a high level of self-esteem. A person from within an economically disadvantaged subgroup might not place the same value on economic success as someone from a different background or might have lower aspirations in relation to their economic standing, so their self-esteem might not suffer so much if they did not achieve economic success.

STEREOTYPES AND SELF-ESTEEM

A possible extension of this is the notion that even if discrimination in itself is not a statistically significant factor in your *level* of self-esteem, it may be a factor in the *type* of issues that affect your self-esteem. For example, as indicated above, in reporting their experiences in relation to self-esteem, women tend to focus more on other people's acceptance or rejection of them whereas men tend to focus more on experiences of success and failure. It seems plausible to suggest that this may relate to societal stereotypes – if from an early age women are encouraged to place particular value on relationships whereas men are encouraged more to attribute value to achieving tasks, then each gender's self-esteem level may be more likely to rise and fall in relation to that particular stereotype.

SEXUALITY AND SELF-ESTEEM

In terms of sexuality, the situation may be different from that of gender, culture or race because of the fact that your sexuality is not always as visible as your gender, culture or race unless you choose to make it known. People usually are brought up within a culture of which they are part and have close relationships with people of the same race and culture. Similarly, it is common to have a network of relationships with people of the same gender. On the other hand, if you are gay or lesbian, until you make a decision to come out as lesbian or gay (if you decide to do so) you may find yourself in a situation where the majority of people around you are heterosexual and the frame of reference which you are expected to relate to is predominantly that of heterosexual people.

DEALING WITH NEGATIVE STEREOTYPES ABOUT YOURSELF

Back in chapter 2 of this book we looked at some possible thinking patterns that might cause difficulties for self-esteem (pages 82–90). Two of these were 'Labelling people and situations' and '"Must", "should" and "ought" thoughts'. These two categories give a route to helping you to deal with issues relating to stereotypes that might be affecting your level of self-esteem.

try it now EXPLORING LABELS

Complete the exercise below to explore how stereotypes may have affected your own self-esteem negatively and to respond appropriately if they have.

1. How would you describe yourself if you were asked to classify yourself in terms of the kinds of group(s) that you belong to? For example, you might say 'white' or 'black' or 'Asian' or 'a gay man' or 'a working-class woman' or any combination of these or a different classification altogether – use the classification which seems most natural to you.

2. What views did the influential people in your life when you were a child or teenager give you about the label/group you have given as your answer to 1 and about how people within that group *should* act or behave? Write those views down (whether positive or negative) and whose views they were (father, mother, teacher, etc.). For each of the negative views, create a balancing thought to counter it or put it in perspective (you can use any of the techniques described in chapter 2 to help with this) and write that down.

3. What views did the influential people in your life when you were a child or teenager have about the *worth* of people within the group you have given as your answer to 1? Write those views down (whether positive or negative) and whose views they were (father, mother, teacher, etc.). For each of the negative views, create a balancing thought to counter it or put it in perspective (again, you can use any of the techniques described in chapter 2 to help with this) and write that down.

Note: If you find it difficult to come up with answers to the above questions, then you can alternatively try to identify *limiting beliefs* about yourself or who you should be via any of the techniques described in chapter 1 (pages 42–6). You may find that some of those limiting beliefs have a component that relates to how someone of your gender/culture/race/sexuality should or should not behave. You can adapt the questions above to explore how you might have come to hold those limiting beliefs.

case study   MAX: EXPLORING LABELS

Max completes the exercise above and comes up with the following answers:

1. *How would you describe yourself if you were asked to classify yourself in terms of the kinds of group(s) that you belong to?*

    Max: 'I am a gay, upper-class man from a privileged background.'

2. *What views did the influential people in your life when you were a child or teenager give you about the label/group you have given as your answer to 1 and about how people within that group should act or behave? Write those views down (whether positive or negative) and whose views they were (father, mother, teacher, etc.). For each of the negative views, create a balancing thought to counter it or put it in perspective and write that down.*

    Max's analysis:

    View: 'Gay men should keep their sexual tendencies to themselves.'
    Person who held that view: Father
    Balancing thought: 'It is natural for me to be gay. I can decide how I want to express that or not as I feel appropriate. My father held his views because of his own background and ignorance. I don't agree with them.'

View: 'If you have privilege you should make a success of yourself.'
Person who held that view: Father, teachers
Balancing thought: 'I can set personal objectives relating to what is important to me. If there is an area where I want to be successful I will try to achieve success but I accept that I may not succeed.'

View: 'You are an interesting individual whatever your sexuality or class.'
Person who held that view: Mother
Balancing thought: N/A (no need for a balancing thought as the view isn't negative)

3. *What views did the influential people in your life when you were a child or teenager have about the worth of people within the group you have given as your answer to 1? Write those views down (whether positive or negative) and whose views they were (father, mother, teacher, etc.). For each of the negative views, create a balancing thought to counter it or put it in perspective and write that down.*

Max's analysis:

View: 'Gay men are embarrassing to others.'
Person who held that view: Father
Balancing thought: 'I am sorry that my father holds that view but it says more about him than about me. I am a lively affectionate person. I have some faults but who doesn't!'

View: 'Gay people often have an interesting perspective to communicate.'

Person who held that view: Mother
Balancing thought: N/A (no need for a balancing thought as the view isn't negative)

USEFUL TIP

Another way to challenge a negative stereotype about how you should be or behave as a person falling within a particular category of people is to think of alternative possible beliefs about the group which are more positive or less dogmatic. Explore those possible alternatives in a way similar to the way in which you might explore alternatives to limiting beliefs about yourself (see chapter 1, pages 48–52).

THE BACKGROUND TO YOUR OWN SELF-ESTEEM

Some of the principles above applying to stereotypes and labels can also be extended or adapted to apply to negative messages you receive from others about yourself which may not fall into any general classifications such as gender, race or sexuality but which nonetheless have a negative impact on you.

The possible causes of low levels of self-esteem mentioned earlier in this chapter are precisely that: *possible* causes. Similarly, the possible classifications of groups mentioned in the preceding pages are *possible* classifications, not the only ones. You are most likely to be able to recognize the reasons for your own level of self-esteem (whether it is high or low) from your memories of previous experiences and the messages that consciously or unconsciously, rightly or wrongly, were transmitted to you from them.

Beliefs don't grow on trees. They are learned from experience and from the messages you are given by others. If you are continually told by someone important to you that you lack certain qualities or have certain negative characteristics, or that you will not achieve very much, or that you should not do certain things, then you may start to believe those things.

Conversely, if those close to you give you *positive* messages, telling you for example that you are worthwhile, you are loved, you are entitled to have opinions, then these are likely to be helpful to your self-esteem.

try it now IDENTIFYING NEGATIVE AND POSITIVE MESSAGES FROM PAST EXPERIENCE

Answer the questions below to reflect on influences or situations in childhood or adulthood which resulted in you being given negative or positive messages about yourself, which may have contributed to your current level of self-esteem.

Note: If you have experienced traumatic abusive experiences in your life and are concerned that answering the questions (or any others in this book) may bring back distressing or hurtful memories of an extreme nature, then you may want to skip this particular exercise or else do it an environment where there is someone who can provide appropriate support to you if needed.

Childhood: Who were the most important people for you in your childhood (parents, siblings, teachers, friends, etc.)? What were the environments, situations or experiences that had most influence on how you developed (home, school, etc.)?

(a) First, write down below any **positive messages** about you and your potential that you gained from these important people, environments or situations.

(b) Next, write down any **negative messages** about you and your potential that you gained from these important people, environments or situations.

(c) Do any of those negative messages still influence your behaviour and thoughts today? If so, create balancing thoughts for them or use some of the techniques from later on in this chapter.

Adulthood: Who have been the most important people in your adult life and what have been the situations or experiences that have influenced you most as an adult?

(a) First, write down below any **positive messages** about you and your potential that you have gained from these important people and situations?

(b) Next, write down any **negative messages** about you and your potential that you have gained from these important people and situations.

(c) Do any of those negative messages still influence your behaviour and thoughts today? If so, create balancing thoughts for them or use some of the techniques from later on in this chapter.

DEALING WITH NEGATIVE MESSAGES FROM YOUR PAST

If doing the above exercise reveals some negative messages from your past that are still haunting you, then you now have a simple explanation of some of the potential causes of your low self-esteem, which you can use to help you move forward. The way to do this when you catch yourself thinking that negative message about yourself is to *remind yourself of the origin of it and then create a balancing thought* to evaluate that negative message in a more constructive way and remind yourself of that balancing thought at appropriate times. An example is given in the case study below.

case study CHRISTINE: DEALING WITH NEGATIVE MESSAGES FROM THE PAST

Christine is a successful professional in her early thirties with a number of good, close friends and a variety of interests, but she frequently puts herself down and finds it difficult to see worth in things that she does, although her opinions are highly valued by others and her friends see her as a warm and generous person.

Christine completes the exercise above, identifying messages from her past experience. It crystallizes for her that one of the likely explanations of her feelings of worthlessness and of not being good enough is that when she was young her parents seldom complimented her and often criticized her.

Christine uses the technique of asking herself what she might say to a friend in her situation (page 78) to create a balancing thought that she can remind herself of when she has that feeling of not being good enough, to help put the negative message in context. Her balancing thought refers to the explanation and then counters it in a simple way, saying:

'It is understandable that you might think of yourself as not being good enough because of the negative messages that you received from your parents when you were younger. In fact, you are highly valued by your friends and successful in your work.'

Christine finds that repeating the statement to herself at appropriate times takes the edge off the stress that she feels when she is being self-critical.

ACKNOWLEDGING YOUR LOW SELF-ESTEEM

There is often a paradox in relation to negative thoughts and low self-esteem that the more you try to fight against it, the worse it can get or the harder it can seem. As Christine's example shows, part of the secret of dealing with low self-esteem is to take it in your stride if you can – rather than try to fight it or deny it in a confrontational way. It is more likely to help you if you can acknowledge it, explain it in simple terms and then make a practical comment that puts it in perspective or addresses the distorted thinking patterns that are involved in your negative thoughts about yourself.

PUTTING LOW SELF-ESTEEM IN CONTEXT

It is important to realize that self-esteem is only one aspect of you! This chapter is entitled *Understand Yourself* and while understanding where your self-esteem (or low self-esteem) originates from is part of that process of understanding yourself, it is not the whole process. If you can build up a picture of you and your values and characteristics which is broader than just seeing yourself in terms of self-esteem then this can help you to develop your potential in a healthy way.

try it now

BUILDING UP A PICTURE OF YOURSELF – FIVE STEPS

There are many ways of helping you to build a more rounded picture of yourself, your values and your aspirations. Here is a five-step process that you can follow to start building up that more complex picture.

Step 1: Identify some characteristics and values that are important to you

(a) Read through the list below of some characteristics that people value, then write down up to five of the listed values and characteristics that you would most like to demonstrate and embody in the way that you live (not necessarily in order of priority). The list is only a guideline. If you can think of something which is not on the list or if you would like to use a different word for what is listed then feel free to do so.

List of possible positive characteristics and values

Appreciation of others · Artistic ability · Awareness of environment · Assertiveness · Balance · Being part of a community · Being in a team · Capacity to change and develop · Chilling out · Collaborating with others · Connecting with people · Creativity · Excitement · Financial management · Family commitment · Freedom · Friendship · Fun · Generosity · Helping others · Honesty · Honour · Humour · Independence · Individuality · Intelligence · Integrity · Intimacy · Kindness · Learning from experience · Looking after myself · Love · Musical ability · Networking · Not taking myself too seriously · Organizational skills · Physical health · Physical fitness · Relaxed approach and attitude · Reliability · Religious lifestyle · Risk-taking · Self-awareness · Self-expression · Sensuality · Sexuality · Sharing · Solitude · Social conscience · Standing up for rights · Spirituality · Stability · Success · Understanding

(b) Write down for yourself an example of a situation, event or incident in your life in which you feel you demonstrated one or more of your selected values or characteristics, describing what happened and which of the values or characteristics it demonstrated.

Step 2: What kind of person do you want to be?

(a) How do you think you currently come across to people?

Insert your own name at the beginning of the below sentence, then complete the rest of the sentence quickly, imagining how others might describe you:

.... is the type of person who ....

....

....

(b) How did you used to come across to people?

Would people have given the same answer to the above question about you if asked it two to three years ago (or some other significant period in the past)? If the answer would have been different, indicate what it might have been at that time by completing the sentence below, again inserting your own name at the beginning of the sentence:

.... used to be the type of person who ....

....

....

(c) What kind of person do you want to be?

Now think about the type of person that you would like to be – this may be similar to one of the above statements or on the other hand it may be something completely different! Complete the sentence below:

I would like to be the type of person who ....
....
....

Step 3: Create an epitaph for yourself!

Imagine that someone is writing your epitaph. What would you like them to write? Write the epitaph down, keeping it succinct (say, one or two sentences). I hope that this epitaph won't be needed for a long time, but thinking about it can help you to identify what is important to you!

Step 4: Remind yourself of your affirmations

Now look back to chapter 1 and read through the affirmations that you created about yourself (page 28).

Step 5: Create a character description of yourself

Finally, look back through the previous steps and try to create a character description of yourself which gives a rounded picture of you that you can remind yourself of when you have a tendency to see yourself in a narrow way. Your character description may just be one paragraph or it may be several paragraphs. Try to write it in a constructive, positive way so that it is a recognition of your values, aspirations and identity. Write it in the third person, at least in the first instance, imagining that you are a friendly third party looking at yourself and giving an honest but constructive account.

When you create your character description in this way it is important that in the first instance you write it from the viewpoint of a friendly third party. If any of your thoughts about the kind of person you want to be (step 2c above) are driven by a wish to be what you think *others* would want you to be or what you *ought* to be, then using the viewpoint of a friendly third party to create your character description can help you to see that you are placing unreasonable or perfectionist demands on yourself.

case study

DOUG: CREATING A CHARACTER DESCRIPTION

Doug works as an actuary, a job which has helped him to earn a reasonable income and support a family. In working hard to help support his family, he has sacrificed some personal interests that he might have liked to explore if he had time – particularly painting, which he was good at when he was younger. When his marriage breaks up he starts to feel disillusionment with what he has done with his life and his self-esteem takes a knock. He uses the five-step process described above to build up a more complex picture of himself and produces the following personal statement:

> Doug is the type of man who doesn't suffer fools gladly but he has an honest heart and is committed to doing the best for his family. When he dies, he would like to be remembered as someone who enjoyed work and life to the full and added value to the lives of others. He has a creative streak which hasn't yet found full expression. He is caring and generous. He is independent and travelled a lot when he was younger. He regrets that some relationships haven't worked out as well as he would have liked but values the important relationships that he does

have. He would like to live a simpler life, less cluttered and less money-focused, and to develop some of his personal interests more when he gets the opportunity.

The point of doing the character description exercise is to build up a fuller picture of yourself, to help you to see that although your self-esteem is a part of you it is not the whole of you. If you think of your life as a journey then it is a journey that is not yet finished. If you suffer from low self-esteem, that can lead you to believe that you are stuck in a certain place on that journey. Doing the character description and the exercises related to it can help you to move forward in that journey as you see yourself in a wider and fuller way and start to build some aspirations from the wider picture of yourself, your values and your wishes.

try it now

Once you have created your character description and its related exercises, ask yourself if there are any particular aspirations which you want to work towards in the next six months, bearing in mind what you have identified about yourself in terms of your values and characteristics and how you see yourself. Set yourself at least one *reasonably achievable* action that you can commit to do or start doing within a specific time frame to help you start moving towards any of the aspirations you identify. In Doug's case, having identified in his character description that he wants to develop some of his personal interests, he might for example set himself the action of doing a painting within a specified time that seems reasonable for him, or joining an evening class to pursue that interest.

THE PAYOFFS OF LOW SELF-ESTEEM

Part of the process of understanding yourself in relation to self-esteem also involves understanding what payoffs you may be getting – or think that you are getting – from having low self-esteem. From the outside looking at someone with low self-esteem it is often easy to identify potential benefits that would ensue for them if they were to increase their self-esteem (for example, in chapter 1 I listed some advantages of having a reasonable level of self-esteem compared to having a low level of self-esteem (page 13), such as feeling better about yourself and being able to engage in relationships more constructively). However, if you are a person who has low self-esteem there may be *perceived* payoffs from having low self-esteem which are actually holding you back from doing things that might improve your self-esteem. Consider the case study below:

case study
SIOBHAN: PERCEIVED PAYOFFS OF LOW SELF-ESTEEM

Siobhan works as a social worker in a team. She is a very experienced member of the team. She has a good awareness of professional issues and is well respected by her colleagues. When a post of Senior Practitioner becomes vacant in the team, she is interested in applying for it, but a voice in her head keeps telling her she is not good enough and she hesitates. One of her colleagues encourages her to go for the job and she explains that she doesn't think she is good enough. The colleague counters this by giving examples and evidence to support her view that Siobhan is competent and capable of fulfilling the Senior Practitioner role. Siobhan then explains that there are a number of worries she has about what might happen if she went for the role:

- She might not get the role and would then be disappointed.

- Other members of the team might think she was arrogant in going for the job.

- She might get the job and then find it too hard or make a fool of herself.

In this example, there is a perceived payoff for Siobhan in having low self-esteem in that it protects her from taking risks which might result in shame or stress. Another related payoff of having low self-esteem for her is that she doesn't have to contemplate changes that might upset her equilibrium. She knows what it is like to have low self-esteem, but she is not sure that having higher self-esteem will be better for her. Maybe it will turn her into a different person from what she is now, she thinks, and she is not sure if she wants that or how her friends will react.

It is important that you identify any perceived payoffs that there may be for you in having low self-esteem. For each perceived payoff, reflect on whether there is a counter argument. Siobhan's list of perceived payoffs and the counter arguments for each might look like this:

Payoff of having low self-esteem: I don't need to take risks which might turn out badly.

Counter argument: If I don't take any risks then I miss out on a lot of potential benefits. It's better to assess how serious the risks are and whether the potential benefits outweigh them rather than to risk nothing.

Payoff of having low self-esteem: Low self-esteem is part of my identity – if I change, I may lose the essence of me and my friends may desert me!

Counter argument: So long as I don't become arrogant, having better self-esteem will help me to develop my potential. At the moment my low self-esteem is restricting me from doing that. My good friends will be pleased for me if I develop my potential.

try it now

If you have low self-esteem, then consider and list the possible payoffs of low self-esteem for you, then write down the counter arguments against each payoff, as in the example above.

DEALING WITH FEAR OF WHAT PEOPLE MIGHT THINK OF YOU

If your low self-esteem is linked to a fear of making a fool of yourself or of offending people then you may find that using a 'graded exposure' approach helps you to overcome that fear:

key term

Graded exposure is where you try out the behaviour you are avoiding or are fearful about in gradual steps, gradually building up the steps if you meet with some initial success. This approach is consistent with the techniques and exercises recommended by Aaron Beck for dealing with anxiety, for example, in his book *Anxiety Disorders and Phobias*.

A typical example of someone using a graded exposure approach would be a situation where you are worried about meeting people because of what they might think of you. It can be helpful to list aspects of your behaviour that you know relate to avoiding risks and then write down alternative behaviours you can try out. Such a list might look something like this:

Risk-averse behaviour: Making an excuse not to go to meet a group of people I don't know because I worry about what they will think of me

Alternative behaviour to try out: Choose to go to meet the group for a short period of time rather than not at all

Risk-averse behaviour: Avoiding eye contact with people

Alternative behaviour to try out: Consciously make eye contact with at least two different people in a social gathering

Risk-averse behaviour: Staying silent when I am in a group of people I don't know

Alternative behaviour to try out: Choose to say something to at least one person in the group before I leave

Risk-averse behaviour: Making a false excuse and leaving a gathering early

Alternative behaviour to try out: Decide not to leave until at least two others have left the gathering

In line with the graded exposure idea, you may find it helpful to order your suggested alternative behaviours and try out the least difficult first.

try it now

If you think that avoiding taking risks is part of your low self-esteem then create a list like the one above identifying risk-averse behaviours you have a tendency towards and specifying alternatives. Choose the least difficult alternative to try out first and see if the results are as you anticipated.

MINDFULNESS PRACTICE FOR SELF-AWARENESS

One approach to self-awareness that can be helpful to people who are struggling with self-esteem issues or negative thoughts is the practice of mindfulness. This is a modern expansion of the Hindu and Buddhist traditions of meditation. Mindfulness is about:

- Calming your mind

- Focusing on the present moment

- Achieving greater stillness, tranquillity and contentment.

In the second half of the 20th century the Vietnamese Buddhist monk Thich Nhat Hanh wrote a series of popular books, including the bestselling book *The Miracle of Mindfulness*, which brought to a Western audience many of the principles of Zen Buddhism and simple meditation practices. Others such as Dr Jon Kabat-Zinn at the University of Massachusetts Medical School have used mindfulness techniques to treat people who are chronically ill or experiencing stressful thoughts.

The practice of mindfulness can be highly relevant to self-esteem issues because of the stream of unchecked negative thoughts that may well run through your head if you experience low self-esteem. There are two aspects to practising mindfulness:

- Basic meditation practice

- Mindfulness in your daily life.

Basic meditation practice: Meditation may sound daunting but in its simplest form it is about helping your mind to focus and be still. This is particularly relevant to self-esteem issues where you may find that your mind is preoccupied by anxieties or self-critical thoughts. One possible way of practising meditation is as follows:

1. Allocate a period of time one day when you are going to try out meditation – perhaps ten or twenty minutes, although it could be as short as five minutes. If possible, find a quiet place where you will be better able to focus without distractions.

2. Sit or kneel with your back straight and relax your shoulders (if your health or physique prevents you adopting this posture then find an alternative posture that is comfortable for you).

3. Close your eyes.

4. Breathe slowly and seek if possible to breathe from your diaphragm (in which case your stomach will rise and fall as you breathe) rather than your upper chest area – you can place a hand on your stomach if you wish, to feel it rise and fall.

5. Count each breath – for your first breath count 'one' in your mind as you breathe in, then 'one' again as you breathe out. For your second breath count 'two' in your mind as you breathe in and then 'two' again as you breathe out. Continue through to ten, then start again on one.

6. Continue this for the set period you have decided on.

7. During the process focus your attention on the counting. It is likely that you will find your mind wandering into thoughts on other things – if and when that happens, just try to draw it back gently to focus on your counting. Try not to criticize yourself if your mind wanders (it is natural), just try to refocus on your counting.

8. At the end of your allotted time period gently finish your meditation, opening your eyes and looking around you to reorient yourself. If you can, carry any feelings of calm through into your next activity and the rest of the day.

Meditation can help you to detach yourself from the oppressive burden of stressful thoughts and to cope with them better. It has most beneficial effects if you practise it regularly. The above suggested instructions encourage you to set aside time for meditation but you can also practise observing your breathing in a similar way in other situations where you are aware that you are experiencing stressful or negative thoughts.

Mindfulness in your daily life: If you find that meditation practice is helpful for you, you may also discover that applying the general principle of taking your time can help you to be able to cope better with the rush of life or the negative energy of self-critical thoughts. Focus on the tasks at hand and gently draw your mind back to a task without judging yourself if your thoughts stray.

Many of us get into a routine of feeling that we have to rush about or achieve certain results. If this applies to you then you may find that sometimes taking things a bit more slowly and focusing on an activity without feeling that you have to achieve particular results helps you to relax and takes away some of the inner stresses created by anxious, critical or negative thoughts. In *The Miracle of Mindfulness* Thich Nhat Hanh gives an example of someone washing the dishes in a hurry to try and get it done as quickly as possible and contrasts it with the mindful way of washing the dishes (which he prefers), which involves focusing on what you are doing and on your breath and experiences and taking your time. He also suggests that you set aside one day a week as a day of mindfulness, when you aim to take things slowly and focus on each task in a relaxed, mindful way.

try it now

Commit to trying out the simple meditation practice outlined above at a specific time this week and/or set aside a day for mindfulness. Afterwards reflect on how you felt during and after the experience and consider whether it might be something you want to do regularly.

REMEMBER

Very few people (if any) meditate perfectly – it is a discipline that takes time to learn. Don't be hard on yourself if your mind wanders while meditating – just try to draw yourself back to the focus of your meditation.

CREATING A SELF-ESTEEM JOURNAL

If the idea of meditating or practising mindfulness doesn't appeal to you and you would prefer a different approach, then an alternative way of getting in touch with your feelings and developing self-awareness in a constructive way is to create a self-esteem journal.

Keeping a journal of this nature involves:

- Keeping personal notes of reflections and activities

- Expressing your thoughts and feelings in the journal

- Following a chosen structure or method in your journal

- Treating your journal as a special record of your own.

The above features are important. The type of journal I am talking about is not just a random outpouring of your thoughts or feelings (which may be helpful as a release but can also become unproductive); it is a document which helps you to:

- Become more self-aware and identify problematic patterns that you may be repeating and/or helpful patterns

- Address problematic patterns

- Treat yourself with respect

- Make positive changes.

USING A JOURNAL TO TACKLE NEGATIVE INNER VOICES

You can use a journal to replace negative inner voices in your mind with more nurturing voices to help build up a healthier, more positive picture of yourself if you are prone to seeing yourself in a negative way. Here is how you might do this:

Step 1: Get yourself a notebook, file or other record-keeping system which you are going to use as your personal journal. Keep it somewhere safe and secure as it is your private document. Commit to making journal entries for two weeks on a regular basis – for example, you might commit to writing ten to fifteen minutes every day, ideally at a regular time.

Step 2: Start writing the journal on a daily basis. In the first instance just write about what you are thinking and feeling at the time – express your concerns, wishes, feelings, thoughts and reflections. You can even write down your reflections on the fact that you are writing a diary if you want or if you get stuck! Write the journal in the first person ('I feel …', 'I think …'). As you write you can reflect on:

- Any immediate concerns

- Things that are going well for you or hopes

- Things that are not going well for you or frustrations and anxieties

- Any apparent patterns in your life, positive or negative, or things that you want to change

- How you act in certain situations and how you think and feel

- Any achievements or positives in the day.

Step 3: After a week, look back at your journal and if there are a number of self-critical or negative statements in the journal, try to identify the characteristics of the negative statements:

- Is there a pattern to the kind of negative statements that come up?

- What is the nature of the critical voice or voices – does it have a particular tone? Does it seem male or female? Do you associate it with any voices from your past or your present? When do you think you might first have heard that kind of statement about you, who might have made it and in what setting?

Step 4: Commit to challenging and replacing the negative voices next week when you write your journal. You can *challenge* negative voices each time you write down a negative thought or criticism in your journal by:

- Imagining what you would say to a best friend who was expressing that negative thought and writing down that response in your diary next to the self-critical or negative thought; *or*

- If you have identified the negative voice as being that of someone you know, ask yourself what issues or reasons they may have prompting them to speak like that and record that in your journal.

- Recording in the journal any evidence which suggests that the negative voice is inaccurate or too extreme.

You can *replace* negative or self-critical reflections in your self-esteem journal by:

- Remembering someone past or present who is supportive to you, imagining them being with you and writing down in your journal positive comments that they might make in response to the negative statement.

- Imagining yourself in the role of a loving supportive parent to yourself and in that role writing down what you would say in response to the negative comment.

Step 5: If you find the process you have followed in step 4 helpful then continue it each week for as long as you find it helpful.

try it now

If you think that using a journal might be useful for you then try completing a self-esteem journal for the next two weeks following the steps described above.

You can find similar and additional ideas for creating helpful self-esteem journals in different ways in Alison Waines' book *The Self-Esteem Journal* (2004).

REMEMBER: KEY IDEAS FROM CHAPTER 4

Some of the key ideas to remember from chapter 4 are:

- Certain parenting styles can contribute to a child's low self-esteem.

- Experiences of abuse, neglect or rejection can lead to low self-esteem.

- Correlations between *levels* of self-esteem and issues of discrimination are not clear cut.

- Societal, cultural or gender-related expectations and other stereotypes may contribute to the *types* of issues that affect your self-esteem most.

- Negative stereotypical labels that you believe about yourself (whatever their cause) may impact adversely on your self-esteem. You can use balancing thoughts to put them in perspective.

- If you have a negative self-image you can help to balance it by creating a more positive and realistic character description of yourself.

- To help you address low self-esteem it is important to identify any payoffs that having low self-esteem gives you and to challenge flawed thinking about those payoffs.

- Mindfulness techniques or creating a self-esteem journal can help you to deal with negative thoughts and feelings arising from a poor self-image.

CHAPTER 5

Empower yourself

'The awakened sages call a person wise when all his
undertakings are free from anxiety about results'
— *The Bhagavad Gita*, 4:19
(translation by Eknath Easwaran)

THREE WAYS OF RELATING TO OTHER PEOPLE

It is sometimes said that there are three basic ways in which you can interact with others: passively, assertively or aggressively. Empowering yourself is about acting assertively.

Passive behaviour is a type of behaviour which is characteristic of someone seeking above all to avoid conflict. If this is a form of behaviour that you show then it is likely that whatever your own feelings, you may allow others to make choices and decisions for you or to take advantage of your goodwill.

Looking back to the threefold classification of people's self-esteem and valuations of themselves that I introduced at the start of the first chapter of this book (1. person with low self-esteem; 2. person with reasonable self-esteem; 3. arrogant or conceited person), you may agree that *passive* behaviour is most likely to be associated with low self-esteem. If you don't value yourself and doubt your own abilities and judgements, you may have a tendency to give in to the views of others or to avoid contesting them or making decisions for yourself.

Assertive behaviour: Acting assertively involves being capable of expressing your own needs, wishes and feelings clearly in a manner which is constructive and which allows others the opportunity to express their own. You can make decisions for yourself but you are also good at taking account of the views and opinions of others and acting with respect.

Again looking back to the threefold classification of people's self-esteem and valuations of themselves from the first chapter, I would suggest that if you have a *reasonable* level of self-esteem, you are more likely to be able to act in an assertive way. You are not excessively worried about what other people think or how you look to them or whether you are capable but nor do you dismiss the views and feelings of others or overestimate your own abilities. You achieve a reasonable middle path to the best of your ability.

Aggressive behaviour is at the other extreme from passive behaviour. Someone who acts aggressively will express their own needs and wants freely but often without thought for the feelings of others and sometimes in a loud or intimidating manner. If you fall into the third category of the original classification relating to self-esteem in chapter 1 (being arrogant or conceited) then you may well be prone to aggressive behaviour.

Sometimes people also talk of 'passive-aggressive' behaviour, which is a kind of masked or silent aggressiveness. It essentially involves being non-cooperative or non-compliant but not expressing your opposition in a clear verbal way. A person who is 'passive-aggressive' may sometimes *appear* to be complying or passive, while actually undermining or sabotaging another person. Acting in a sulky way, obstructing indirectly or creating confusion to avoid doing something would be examples of passive-aggressive behaviour.

ASSERTIVENESS – THE MIDDLE WAY

In chapter 1 I suggested that the middle category of having a reasonable level of self-esteem was the one I would encourage you to aim for. Similarly, here I would suggest that the middle category of acting assertively is the one I would generally encourage you to aim for rather than either of the two extremes of being passive or being aggressive.

A person who is assertive might be described as someone who:

- Expresses their views clearly and articulately without being aggressive

- Stands up for their own and other people's rights in a reasonable and clear way

- Allows other people a reasonable opportunity to express their opinions without allowing them to dominate a conversation

- Has the courage to express their own feelings, even about difficult issues, in a way which is respectful and honest.

Key elements of assertiveness are:
- Clarity
- Reasonableness
- Honesty
- Respect.

FEATURES OF ASSERTIVE BEHAVIOUR

Often the following are highlighted as features of assertive behaviour:

- Acknowledging when you are expressing your own feelings or wishes, by using personal statements, such as: 'I would like it if ...'; 'I prefer ...'; 'I feel ...'

- Making it clear when you are stating an opinion or point of view, for example using phrases such as: 'In my opinion …'; 'My personal view is that …'; 'My impression is that …'

- Asking about others' views of situations or their feelings in an open way which allows them to articulate their views if they want to, for example by using open questions such as: 'What do you think of …?'; 'What are your views on …?'; 'How do you feel about …?'; 'What would you like …?'

NON-VERBAL ASPECTS OF ASSERTIVE BEHAVIOUR

As well as words, your actions may contribute to you behaving in a reasonable, assertive way rather than in a passive or aggressive way. Non-verbal behaviour which can contribute to being assertive in a reasonable way include:

- Speaking in a friendly warm tone without overdoing it by being condescending

- Using friendly but not overly aggressive gestures to illustrate your feelings – for example, by gesturing in an illustrative but not threatening way with your hands

- Looking at others where appropriate but trying not to invade their personal space by getting *too* close inappropriately.

THE BENEFITS OF BEING ASSERTIVE

There are many potential benefits to being assertive, including:

- Feeling better about yourself

- Feeling more confident

- Being able to relax more

- Having greater awareness of your own needs and a greater ability to meet them

- Being able to create personal and professional goals instead of putting everyone or everything else first

- Participating in honest, constructive relationships where you and others can develop understanding and respect and solve problems together.

REMEMBER

Assertiveness is *not* about forcing your views on others or dominating a conversation, nor is it about allowing others to dominate you. The first of these two extremes would usually be regarded as *aggressive* behaviour and the second would usually be regarded as *passive*. (Those types of behaviour are illustrated further in the two case studies below.)

case study   ANGIE: PASSIVE BEHAVIOUR

Angie has a low level of self-esteem. She doesn't believe that she is very good at most things and she worries about making a fool of herself or annoying other people. Angie has the following tendencies:

- She quite often keeps silent when someone says something she disagrees with or doesn't like rather than expressing her opinion.

- She sometimes says that she agrees with something even though she doesn't as she doesn't want to cause a disturbance or create conflict.

- She quite often agrees to take on tasks or do things when asked even if she doesn't really have the time.

When Angie thinks about why she acts passively she realizes that there are a number of perceived or short-term benefits that she is seeking from acting passively. In the short term, she often:

- Avoids confrontation and argument

- Avoids being criticized by others

- Feels that she is acting selflessly or in the way that she thinks she 'should' do.

When she reflects further on the perceived payoffs of acting passively, Angie realizes that actually they are only short term and they build up or mask other problems. She realizes that:

- Often a confrontation or argument is just postponed – she builds up resentment and is unable to control it coming out later on, or else others do not appreciate what she is really feeling and subsequently are surprised and perplexed when she reacts in a different way.

- Other people do not always respect her for being silent – sometimes she is criticized for not speaking up or not expressing her views.

- Sometimes when she takes on too many tasks, she doesn't complete them and that leads to criticism from others and a feeling on her part that she has let them down.

- She rarely gets the chance to do things that she wants – this leads to her being frequently tired, stressed and sometimes feeling demotivated or powerless.

case study RICHARD: AGGRESSIVE BEHAVIOUR

Richard is a high flyer in his job. However, he is quite arrogant. He manages a team and often behaves towards them in quite a domineering way, not taking account of their views or opinions. He is confident in his own judgement (sometimes overly so, as he is not always right). Richard has a tendency to:

● Shout or speak very loudly

● Tell people what they ought to do or must do

● Put people down or describe their behaviour as unacceptable

● Frequently find faults in others

● State his own opinions as if they were facts which others cannot disagree with or have no right to disagree with.

Richard acts aggressively because he believes that:

● It saves him time.

● It leads to good decisions being made.

● It means everyone in his team knows their role and can therefore perform efficiently.

Richard shuts his eyes to possible problems from his actions. Members of his team tend to say the following:

● It is unpleasant working with him because he shows no respect for anyone.

● He is opinionated and as he never listens to anyone else's view he sometimes gets things wrong which he could have got right if he had listened.

- People are scared to speak to him honestly so he doesn't get full information about issues that could be of interest and concern to him.

- If he continues to act in this way there is going to be a high turnover of staff in his team.

try it now

People do not always fit neatly into categories. Although you can probably see that you have a tendency to fall into one of the categories of behaviour (passive, assertive or aggressive), you may also be able to find examples where you have shown one of the other types. Complete the exercise below to explore your own patterns of behaviour in relation to each type:

Exploring your patterns of behaviour

1. **Passive behaviour:** Do you have a tendency to act passively at times? If so, think of one example of a situation where you acted passively.
   - What perceived payoffs did you hope to get by acting passively?
   - Were the payoffs real or just imagined?

2. **Aggressive behaviour:** Do you have a tendency to act aggressively at times? If so, think of one example of a situation where you acted aggressively.
   - What perceived payoffs did you hope to get by acting aggressively?
   - Were the payoffs real or just imagined?

3. **Assertive behaviour:** Think of one occasion where you acted reasonably assertively.
   - What benefits did you get from acting assertively in the situation?
   - What helped you to act assertively in this situation?

APPROACHES TO BECOMING MORE ASSERTIVE

This book is aimed primarily at helping people with low self-esteem to find ways in which they can build their self-esteem up to a reasonable level. The next part of this chapter describes two methods which you can use to help you become more assertive if you have low self-esteem linked to a tendency to act passively or to put yourself down in the way you relate to others.

ASSERTIVENESS METHODS: 1. THE DEAL METHOD

Assertiveness is primarily about the way you communicate with and act towards other people and how you handle problematic situations. The first method for helping you to act more assertively relates to how you can deal with the kind of situation where someone is doing something that is creating problems for you or seems unfair, and you want to raise it with them but are not sure how. I use the acronym 'DEAL' to indicate the steps that you can take in this situation. DEAL stands for:

Describe the situation or behaviour that is troubling you.

Express your feelings and thoughts about it.

Ask for reasonable changes that you feel would help.

Listen and negotiate for a reasonable solution if possible.

The DEAL method builds on four key elements of assertive behaviour which I mentioned near the start of this chapter (page 172) – clarity, reasonableness, honesty and respect.

In particular the approach is about *reasonableness*. Remember that it is reasonable for you to express your own wishes and needs in a polite but assertive way and then follow the DEAL method in doing that. Here is an example to show how you might use the method to discuss a difficult issue with someone you know:

case study JEANINE: USING THE DEAL METHOD TO BE MORE ASSERTIVE

Jeanine feels exhausted and resentful because she is doing all the childcare in her household and she would like her partner Simon to help out but she is worried about his reaction if she raises the matter.

How could Jeanine use the DEAL acronym to help her raise this issue with Simon?

Step 1: Describe the situation to the other person

In describing the situation it usually helps to be specific and clear, giving an example of what you are finding to be a problem and trying to be accurate in what you say rather than using emotive or generalized language. Thus rather than say to Simon 'Why do you never help me with looking after the children?' which might receive a hostile reaction, Jeanine could for example say:

> 'I've been thinking about the arrangements for Saturday night and I've realized it may create some problems for me to look after the children then. I was hoping to go out with my friend X because it's her birthday and it won't be possible to if I have to stay at home with the children.'

It is important that you speak in a way that reflects your own natural use of language – don't put on airs and graces! – but the point is to try to be clear and specific: make sure that you express clearly and simply what the problem is.

Step 2: Express your feelings and thoughts about it

Although your feelings may be obvious to you, the person you are speaking to will not necessarily know what they are unless you tell them, so try as best you can to explain to them how the situation is making you feel. Jeanine, for example, might say to Simon:

> 'I feel hurt that you haven't offered to help out in this situation and that I am doing most of the childcare, which is leaving me tired. For example, last week it was me who put the children to bed every night.'

Again, you will want to adapt the actual phrases used to fit your own style and vocabulary, while following the overriding principles:

- Usually it is best to avoid extreme or overly emotional language.

- Keep your statement simple and accurate.

- Express your feelings and indicate what is the basis for them.

- Take ownership of your feelings – i.e. you are acknowledging that this is how you feel, not suggesting that everyone would necessarily feel that way or that you are giving a universal truth.

Step 3: Ask for reasonable changes that you feel would help

Again, remember that the person you are talking to may not be able to read your mind, so if you know what you would like, it is helpful if you can be precise about it, e.g. Jeanine might specifically ask Simon:

> 'Do you think you could look after the children on Saturday night so that I can go out? I can take care of them on Friday if you want to go out then.'

In asking for changes, it is again important to be clear and direct about what you are asking while trying to be polite and not over-personalizing the request with emotive critical descriptions of the other person.

If there are examples when the other person has done what you would like them to do, then one possibility is to start by focusing on these, e.g. Jeanine could say:

'On Wednesday it really helped when you looked after the children for a couple of hours. If you can do a similar thing again I would appreciate it.'

In the interests of reasonableness and balance, make it clear that you are not saying the other person is all bad, by highlighting positives as well as being clear about what you would like them to do differently and why.

Step 4: Listen and negotiate a reasonable solution where possible

Often the other person may have a different perspective on the situation. If you have not voiced your concerns before or have done so in an unassertive way, they may not even be aware of the concerns until you express them clearly.

Alternatively, it is possible that there are reasons or thoughts behind their behaviour and actions which have not occurred to you – for example, Jeanine's partner Simon may actually feel that there are a lot of tasks that he does, which she doesn't help with.

Once you have expressed your thoughts and feelings and what you would like, it is therefore usually important to check out what the other person thinks. Jeanine could do this for example simply by asking Simon 'What do you think?' or 'What are your thoughts about it?'

Once the other person has responded, if they are not fully in agreement with what you have suggested then you can try to explore with them whether an alternative solution is possible. In the example situation, Jeanine can try to explore with Simon:

- What is most important to her in the situation and what is most important to him – is it possible to meet both their priorities (the ideal solution)?

- What alternatives are possible – e.g. could they get a babysitter for the specific instance above and then agree future arrangements?

- In what ways are they both willing to compromise?

There are certain situations in which one or both parties is not willing to compromise. However, if you are in a situation where there might be a possibility of some compromise then it is worth thinking about what areas you might compromise on and how you can find out what the other person might compromise on without too much resentment so that you can reach a mutually acceptable solution. In essence this is about developing negotiation skills. Here are some negotiation tips to think about.

USEFUL TIPS: NEGOTIATION TIPS: PREPARING TO GET A REASONABLE DEAL

The tips below are designed to give you some pointers to how to prepare for effective negotiation or discussion around an issue where there are two or more points of view:

1. Identify for yourself what things you are prepared to compromise on and what things you are not willing to compromise on because they are too important to you.

2. Using your knowledge of the behaviour and personality of the person you are going to be in discussion/negotiation with, give some thought in advance to what they might ask for and how you might respond.

3. Be prepared to listen to what the other person has to say but also think about how you are going to ensure that you get an opportunity to put your point of view and feelings across – in some cases it may be helpful at the outset of the discussion for you to suggest to the other person that you agree to allow each other a few minutes each in turn to express your views without interruption.

4. Prepare for how you may try to move discussion forward once you have both expressed your views – for example, this might involve you summarizing the differences and similarities in each of your views and then trying with the other person to explore (or 'brainstorm') what different possible solutions there might be and what the advantages and disadvantages of these are for each of you.

5. In respect of those aspects where you might compromise, think of possible suggestions that you might make to the other party about what you would like in return from them if you compromise on those aspects.

6. In respect of those aspects where you are not willing to compromise, be clear in your own mind about what the consequences might be if the other person still refuses to meet those 'bottom-line' requests and what you will then do.

7. In most cases you will be hoping that a productive compromise can be reached. However, if your bottom-line requests are not met, then be prepared to act in the way you decided beforehand (under point 6 above). If you are not prepared to carry through this commitment then you may decide that actually what you considered to be a 'non-negotiable' or 'bottom-line' request is actually just a strong preference. It is best to be clear about this in your own mind beforehand if possible.

In the case study of Jeanine above, you can see that under step 3 (ask for reasonable changes) there is already an example of how point 5 in the negotiation tips might be used in her situation to put forward a possible compromise proposal whereby she offers to look after the children on Friday if Simon does so on Saturday. Other points from the negotiation tips above, such as point 3, can also be seen in Jeanine's thoughts about how she might express her thoughts and feelings using steps 1–3 of the DEAL method.

Point 6 in the negotiation tips highlights that it is important to be aware of what you will or won't do if the other person doesn't give you the minimum of what you would like. Hopefully you will not need to implement this but it is important to be clear about it in your own mind.

If you can reach an agreement with the other person, then to avoid misunderstanding, confirm with them what it is and clarify any grey areas – in a formal situation you may also want to make a written note of it and share that with the other person if appropriate.

If you cannot reach a compromise with the other person, then consider what (if any) are the implications for the relationship and what choices you have for the future.

try it now

USE THE DEAL METHOD TO DISCUSS A PROBLEM

Complete the exercise below to help you prepare to raise an issue you are concerned about with someone you know:

1. **Describe the situation**
   Follow the principles described above to formulate one or two sentences that you might use when describing the situation you are concerned about. Keep your description as short and clear as you can and express it in the first person (i.e. beginning 'I').

2. **Express your feelings and thoughts about the situation**
   Now follow the principles described above to formulate one or two sentences that you might use to communicate how you feel about the issue.

3. **Ask for reasonable changes that you feel would help**
   Next, set out in one or two sentences the request that you would like to make or a possible proposal that you feel would improve the situation.

4. **Listen and negotiate a reasonable solution where possible**
   Read through the negotiation tips on pages 184–6 to highlight relevant points for you in trying to reach a compromise or a solution. Make a note of any particularly relevant tips in your situation and how you can apply them.

ASSERTIVENESS METHODS: 2. THE STAR MODEL

The second method for improving assertiveness I call the STAR model. It is of particular help for situations that seem to have a kind of repeating pattern in your life, where you find that you have anxious or negative thoughts of a nature that recurs and holds you back from acting positively or as you would like to.

In chapter 2, I introduced some of the key concepts of cognitive behavioural therapy (CBT), including the ABC model devised by Albert Ellis for addressing problematic feelings created by distorted thought patterns or beliefs. The STAR model that I have devised is based on CBT principles but it adds an additional dimension to Ellis's initial concepts by clearly drawing out *actions* as well as thoughts and feelings. This is particularly helpful for assertiveness issues because often what you want to achieve if you are trying to be more assertive is to *act* differently.

The STAR model analyzes the aspects of a problematic situation, representing them in terms of the acronym 'STAR' and diagrammatically as a four-pointed star:

Situation:

> What is the specific situation or type of situation which may create anxieties for you?

Thoughts and feelings:

> What thoughts go through your mind and what do you say to yourself in the situation?

Actions:

> How do you typically act in the situation, in response to it and in response to your thoughts and feelings?

Results:

> What are usually the results for you of your actions, in practical terms and in terms of how you feel afterwards?

The STAR model

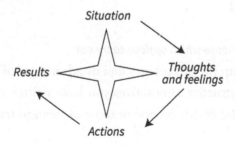

Using the STAR model involves four steps:

Step 1: Describe a typical problem situation using the STAR acronym

Analyze the situation in terms of:

- What the **situation** is where the problem arises

- What your typical **thoughts and feelings** are in that situation

- How you **act** (or avoid acting)

- What the **results** are, both in practical terms and in your resulting thoughts and feelings.

Step 2: Set out possible constructive alternatives

Write down possible things you could try to help deal with potential problems relating to any of the above points. Also think about how you can reward yourself each time you implement one of the constructive alternatives in future as an incentive for you to keep doing it!

Step 3: Choose which options to try out

Weigh up the advantages and disadvantages of each of the constructive alternatives you have written down in step 2 and decide on one or more of them to try out.

Step 4: Try out your selected options and monitor success

Keep a record of what happens when you try out any of the options. Continue with your proposed options if helpful or adjust them if that seems sensible. The idea is to learn from what works and what doesn't and to build on and adjust your techniques for dealing with the situation accordingly.

case study SELIMA: USING THE STAR MODEL

Selima has low self-esteem. She doubts her own abilities and thinks that others must think of her as not having much to contribute to discussions. In her job she often has to attend meetings. When she does so she worries about saying something stupid and as a result she usually does not say very much at all. The end result is often that she then criticizes herself for not contributing and her low self-esteem is reinforced. Selima uses the STAR model to help deal with this pattern of behaviour at meetings and the resultant self-critical thoughts:

Step 1: Describe the situation using the STAR acronym
   Situation: Attending meetings at work

   Thoughts and feelings:
      (Thoughts)
      ● 'What if I make a fool of myself?'
      ● 'They're all cleverer than me.'
      ● 'I never manage to speak well in meetings. I always end up saying something stupid or forgetting what I want to say.'

(Feelings)
- Very anxious and nervous to the point of panic.

Actions:
- Usually, I say very little in the meetings because I get flustered.
- Occasionally I do manage to say something, although not as much as I feel I should.

Results:
(Practical)
- The meeting ends without me having said much and I have not really taken in what was said.
- Other people don't usually make any comment.

(Thoughts and feelings)
- I wonder if everyone else has been thinking how stupid I was at the meeting.
- I feel pathetic and a failure.

Step 2: Set out possible constructive alternatives

Situation – constructive alternatives:
- Try to go with a supportive colleague to a meeting if possible.
- Read the strategies listed below before going to a meeting so that I am prepared.
- Practise a positive visualization exercise to help me build confidence before meetings (**Note:** information about how to practise positive visualization is given later in this chapter on pages 195–7).

Thoughts and feelings – constructive alternatives:
Remind myself that:
- I am not stupid. I just have a particular anxiety about meetings. I can try to overcome that by keeping calm and not exaggerating my faults.
- Nobody is perfect. It's okay to find some things hard. I can try to make it easier by focusing on getting through the first ten minutes of the meeting, then the next ten minutes and so on step by step.
- Some of the people may think I am not very clever, but others know me better and some people won't care as they have their own problems to worry about.
- Try concentrating for fifty per cent of the time – at least that will be an improvement!

Actions – constructive alternatives:
- When in the meeting, speak once at least. Treat anything else as a bonus.
- Congratulate myself as I get through each ten minutes of the meeting.
- In the meeting remind myself that other people may be more worried about themselves.
- If I get flustered and say something which I think is stupid, remind myself that everybody makes mistakes at some time and I am doing my best.

Results – constructive alternatives:
Once the meeting has happened I can't go back in time and change what has happened if I am not happy with it. However, I can:

- Reflect on what went well and what could be improved and make a note of what I can do differently next time and what I can congratulate myself for this time.
- Remind myself that I have done my best and meetings are just not my strong point.
- Take my mind off my anxieties by doing something completely different.

Step 3: Choose which options to try out
Having weighed up the probable consequences and the practicalities of trying to implement the different constructive alternatives, Selima decides first of all to try out the option of practising a positive visualization exercise and the constructive alternatives relating to 'Thoughts and feelings' and 'Actions' for what she can say to herself before and during the meetings she does attend.

Step 4: Try out your selected options and monitor success
Selima tries out her proposed options and records the results:

Period monitored: month of September
Option tried out: Positive visualization (see page 195)
Record of what happened: At first I was a bit sceptical about this but I tried out the visualization technique in advance of two meetings. It definitely helped me to feel and act more confidently in the meetings and to put forward my views when I might not otherwise have done so. However, I feel I need to practise more to get the maximum benefit from the technique. *Updated strategy:* Continue with this strategy but try to practise positive visualizations twice before an important meeting rather than once if I have time, until I feel more comfortable.

Option tried out: Using the constructive 'self-talk' identified in relation to my *thoughts and feelings* and my *actions*

Record of what happened: I felt better through realizing that I do not have to be perfect and that other people may not be paying as much attention to me as I imagine. I still got nervous before one meeting I attended and didn't say as much as others, but I managed to make two contributions which people liked and I am proud of that.

Updated strategy: Continue with 'self talk' before and during meetings to keep me motivated. Also I have now decided to reward myself when I get through a difficult meeting, by going out for a nice lunch with a friendly work colleague after the meeting!

POSITIVE VISUALIZATION

If you have difficulty in believing that you are going to be able to carry out tasks effectively then you can practice positive visualization to help you prepare for the tasks. In the above example, Selima used the technique to help her prepare for meetings. You could also use it in relation to a job interview or a presentation or many other situations that you are nervous about.

To do your positive visualization exercise:

1. Find a quiet place where you can practise the visualization free from any distractions.

2. Do a relaxation exercise for a few minutes to get you into a relaxed frame of mind (see pages 126–9).

3. Imagine yourself entering into the situation or starting on the task that you are anxious about. Use all your senses to help with the visualization: imagine what your surroundings look like, what sounds there are, any smells or tastes or touch-related sensations.

4. Now imagine yourself starting to carry out the task effectively, confidently and successfully. If it helps you to do this, imagine that you are doing it in the same way that someone you know who is good at doing the task would do it, or focus on a positive role model who you admire and imagine yourself acting like them.

5. If you start to feel at all nervous at any point in the process then calm yourself by focusing on your breathing. Reassure yourself that it is okay to get nervous then refocus on the task.

6. Then imagine some potentially problematic situations arising that might throw you off your stride – some unexpected events, or some negative thoughts entering into your mind. When these happen remind yourself of any balancing thoughts that might help to put the negative thoughts in perspective (see chapter 2) and imagine yourself staying calm, dealing with

the difficulty successfully and moving on to the next stage of the task.

7. Imagine yourself completing the task successfully notwithstanding the problems and reaping the benefits at the end. Imagine any positives that will then arise at the end of the process – such as your own feelings of positivity and relaxation and any positive feedback from others.

try it now

If you have a recurring problem situation which reinforces your low self-esteem, use the STAR model method to analyze the situation and to modify the way you deal with it. If relevant and practical, then try practising positive visualization before you implement any strategies you decide on.

REMEMBER: KEY IDEAS FROM CHAPTER 5
Some of the key ideas from chapter 5 are:

• Empowering yourself is about acting assertively rather than passively or aggressively.

• Acting assertively involves expressing your own needs, wishes and feelings clearly in a constructive way which also allows others to express their own.

• The DEAL method is a way of helping you to discuss a troublesome issue with someone. DEAL stands for:

Describe the situation or behaviour that is troubling you.
Express your feelings and thoughts about it.
Ask for reasonable changes that you feel would help.
Listen and negotiate for a reasonable solution if possible.

- The STAR model is a way of addressing anxious patterns that may be preventing you acting assertively. STAR stands for:

  Situation (What is the situation where the problem typically arises?)

  Thoughts and feelings (What are your thoughts and feelings in that situation?)

  Actions (How do you typically act – or avoid acting?)

  Results (What are the results usually – both in practical terms and in terms of your resulting thoughts and feelings?)

  Once you have analyzed a situation using the STAR model, set out possible constructive alternatives for each aspect of the star, choose some options to try out and monitor their success.

- You can use positive visualization to help prepare for specific daunting tasks or occasions more effectively.

Conclusion: Continuing your journey to self-esteem

We have now covered the five areas in the VALUE acronym for helping you on a journey towards a reasonable level of self-esteem:

Value yourself
Accept yourself
Look after yourself
Understand yourself
Empower yourself.

Each chapter has contained exercises and tips to try out. Now that you have finished reading, you may find it helpful to reflect on what has been most useful for you in the ideas I have set out, so that you can put them to use in the most practical and helpful way.

If you are keen to raise your self-esteem further, why not create a project plan to help you towards your destination, focusing on the ideas that you think are most likely to help you personally? You can create your project plan by doing the following:

Step 1: Assess your current level of self-esteem

Complete a questionnaire relating to self-esteem such as the Rosenberg Self-Esteem Scale (page 205)

Make a list of a few outcomes that you would like to move towards: these might include items directly relating to the Rosenberg Self-Esteem Scale such as 'Learning to take a more positive attitude towards myself' or 'Recognizing my good qualities' or they might include other important issues relating to self-esteem for you that you want to address.

Step 2: Set yourself some specific actions to try out or exercises to complete

Look through the parts of the book which you think are most likely to be helpful for you in moving towards your outcomes and select from there a small number of specific actions, exercises or ideas to try out over the next one to two weeks

Work out when you are going to try out the actions, exercises or ideas. Make sure that you set yourself goals in relation to doing them which are 'SMART', i.e.:

Specific

Measurable

Achievable

Realistic and relevant (to what you are trying to achieve overall)

Time framed (say when you are going to do an action or exercise and how many times or for how long).

Step 3: Record your actions in writing on a project plan

- Write down your commitment and plan it with clear goals – this has been shown by research to be helpful to people in moving towards their objectives.

- Give your project plan a name that means something to you – ideally the name will encapsulate a change in your behaviour or way of thinking that you think will help you to move towards your outcomes (so you might for example call it *Value Yourself!* or *Balance* or *Assertive Lisa* or *Dave the Brave* or *Sparkle!* – the more personal the name is to you the better; the main aim is to find a name that is useful and will help to motivate you).

- Keep the project and the project name in your con-sciousness – e.g. by reading the project plan daily or by putting your project name somewhere where you will see it frequently. You can also remind yourself of your project in creative ways if you want, such as by drawing an image of you doing an action on the project plan, or keeping a photo of someone or something that you think may inspire you to pursue the project!

Step 4: Act on your plan

- Try to implement the actions on your project plan and record your progress.

- Update your project plan at regular intervals (say, weekly or fortnightly initially), adding new actions or committing to continue existing actions if appropriate.

- Try to adopt a pragmatic, experimental attitude. If something in your plan works then, unless there is good reason not to, continue with it until you no longer need to; if something in your project plan doesn't seem to work then don't be overly self-critical, just ask yourself why that might be, how you might refine it so that it is achievable or whether to replace it with another action.

Step 5: Review your progress

- After a reasonable period (say three months) assess how far you have come by redoing your initial self-esteem questionnaire to see if any of your answers have changed.

- Reflect on any actions you have taken and whether they have helped you to move towards your desired outcomes.

- Once you have done that, update your project plan and the outcomes in it if required.

try it now

Here is a sample format you can use for your project plan. If you want to adjust the format to make it more interesting for you then please do! Feel free to be creative:

Project: [*INSERT MOTIVATIONAL PROJECT NAME*]

Your name:

Date of start of project:

Outcomes to aim for (medium term):

-

-

-

-

Actions/exercises to do ....

....

When to be carried out ....

....

Record of progress ....

....

Good luck on your journey – and if you can, approach it with a spirit of adventure!

Appendix:
The Rosenberg
Self-Esteem Scale

Below is a list of statements dealing with your general feelings about yourself. For each statement, if you strongly agree, circle SA. If you simply agree, circle A. If you disagree, circle D. If you strongly disagree, circle SD.

1. 'I feel that I'm a person of worth, at least on an equal plane with others.'

   SA　　　　A　　　　D　　　　SD

2. 'I feel that I have a number of good qualities.'

   SA　　　　A　　　　D　　　　SD

3. 'All in all, I am inclined to feel that I am a failure.'

   SA　　　　A　　　　D　　　　SD

4. 'I am able to do things as well as most other people.'

   SA　　　　A　　　　D　　　　SD

5. 'I feel I do not have much to be proud of.'

   SA　　　　A　　　　D　　　　SD

6. 'I take a positive attitude toward myself.'

   SA   A   D   SD

7. 'On the whole I am satisfied with myself.'

   SA   A   D   SD

8. 'I wish I could have more respect for myself.'

   SA   A   D   SD

9. 'I certainly feel useless at times.'

   SA   A   D   SD

10. 'At times I think I am no good at all.'

    SA   A   D   SD

Source: Rosenberg, Morris. 1989. *Society and the Adolescent Self-Image.* Revised edition. Middletown, CT: Wesleyan University Press.

Devised by Dr Morris Rosenberg, the scale was initially used to assess the self-esteem of a sample group of over 5,000 high school children in New York. Since then it has been widely used in a range of settings and locations with a variety of different user groups, including both adults and children, male and female participants.

SCORING YOUR ANSWERS TO THE ROSENBERG SELF-ESTEEM SCALE

Five of the questions focus on self-observations that you are likely to strongly agree with if you have a high level of self-esteem.

The other five questions focus on self-observations that you are likely to strongly agree with if you have a low level of self-esteem.

Therefore use the following system to score your results:

For questions 1, 2, 4, 6 and 7: SA=3, A=2, D=1, SD=0

For questions 3, 5, 8, 9 and 10: SA=0, A=1, D=2, SD=3

USING THE ROSENBERG SELF-ESTEEM SCALE

The lowest score you could achieve on the Rosenberg Self-Esteem Scale would be zero (which would indicate a very low level of self-esteem). The highest score you could achieve would be 30. Most people will be somewhere in between! There are no general rules about what would be a 'normal' score (this may vary depending on the target group taking the test) nor what level counts as 'high' self-esteem and what as 'low' self-esteem.

If you are using the test as a tool to help assess your own self-esteem (or that of someone else) as part of a self-development programme, then you can use it before you start the programme and after an appropriate interval – such as completion of a significant aspect of the programme or completion of the whole programme – to help assess whether the programme has been helpful for you in building your self-esteem.

Additional resources

The books listed below in alphabetical order provide useful information about possible approaches to self-esteem.

Overcoming Low Self-Esteem: A Self-Help Guide Using Cognitive Behavioral Techniques by Melanie Fennel (Robinson, 2009)

Self-Esteem: A Proven Program of Cognitive Techniques for Assessing, Improving and Maintaining Your Self-Esteem by Matthew McKay and Patrick Fanning (New Harbinger Publications, 2000)

Self-Esteem: Research, Theory and Practice by Chris Mruk (Free Association Books, 1999)

Self-Esteem: The Costs and Causes of Low Self-Worth by Nicholas Emler (Joseph Rowntree Foundation, 2001)

Ten Days to Self-Esteem by David D. Burns (Harper, 1993)

The Myth of Self-Esteem: How Rational Emotive Behavior Therapy Can Change Your Life Forever by Albert Ellis (Prometheus Books, 2005)

The Self-Esteem Journal: Using a Journal to Build Self-Esteem by Alison Waines (Sheldon Press, 2004)

The Six Pillars of Self-Esteem by Nathaniel Branden (Bantam, 1995)

Women and Self-Esteem: Understanding and Improving the Way We Think and Feel About Ourselves by Linda Tschirhart Sanford and Mary Ellen Donovan (Penguin Books Ltd, 1993)

AUTHOR'S WEBSITE

Information about life coaching and ebooks on a variety of other self-help topics, such as anxiety, assertiveness, life change and cognitive behavioural therapy techniques, can be found at David Bonham-Carter's life coaching website:

www.davidbonham-carter.com

Index